CW01665294

War Taxation of Incomes, Excess Profits, and Luxuries in Certain Foreign Countries

Elibron Classics
www.elibron.com

Elibron Classics series.

ISBN 0-543-85084-6 (paperback)
ISBN 0-543-85083-8 (hardcover)

This Elibron Classics Replica Edition is an unabridged facsimile of the edition published in 1918, Washington.

WAR TAXATION OF
INCOMES, EXCESS PROFITS, AND LUXURIES
IN CERTAIN FOREIGN COUNTRIES

Prepared in the

LEGISLATIVE REFERENCE DIVISION
LIBRARY OF CONGRESS

Printed for the use of the Committee on Ways and Means

WASHINGTON
GOVERNMENT PRINTING OFFICE
1918

CONTENTS.

INCOME TAX

GREAT BRITAIN.[1]

SYNOPSIS OF INCOME-TAX ACTS, INCLUDING BUDGET PROPOSALS OF 1918.[2]

I. RATES OF TAX.

Normal tax.—Six shillings in the pound sterling (30 per cent). [For taxes on incomes under £2,500 ($12,500), see below, Exemption, abatement, and relief.]

Supertax.—Incomes over £2,500 ($12,500) are subject to a supertax according to the following graduated scale:

Portion of income.		Rate.	
		In the pound.	Per cent
On the first £3,000		s. d.	
First £2,000	First $10,000	0	.....
Next £500	Next $2,500 ($10,000-12,500)	1 0	5
Next £500	Next $2,500 ($12,500-15,000)	1 6	7½
On the fourth £1,000 (£3,000 to £4,000)	Next $5,000 ($15,000-20,000)	2 0	10
On the fifth £1,000 (£4,000 to £5,000)	Next $5,000 ($20,000-25,000)	2 6	12½
On the sixth £1,000 (£5,000 to £6,000)	Next $5,000 ($25,000-30,000)	3 0	15
On the next £2,000 (£6,000 to £8,000)	Next $10,000 ($30,000-40,000)	3 6	17½
On the next £2,000 (£8,000 to £10,000)	Next $10,000 ($40,000-50,000)	4 0	20
On the remainder (above £10,000)	Next $10,000 (above $50,000)	4 6	22½

II. EXEMPTION, ABATEMENT, AND RELIEF.

Exemption.—Incomes not exceeding £130 (about $650) are exempt.

REDUCTION OF AMOUNT TO BE TAXED.

Abatement.—In the case of incomes over £130 and not exceeding £700 ($650 to $3,500) a deduction known as an "abatement" is made before the income-tax rate is applied. This abatement is graduated as follows:

Income.	Abatement.
Exceeding £130 ($650) and not exceeding £400 ($2,000)	£120 ($600)
Exceeding £400 ($2,000) and not exceeding £600 ($3,000)	100 (500)
Exceeding £600 ($3,000) and not exceeding £700 ($3,500)	70 (350)

In the case of incomes exceeding £700 ($3,500) no abatement is made, and the tax is levied on the whole income at the rate applicable thereto.

[1] For the sake of simplicity, $5 has been taken as the approximate equivalent of £1 in converting pounds sterling into dollars.
[2] Amendments to the Finance bill, 1918, made by the House of Commons in Committee of the Whole, June 3, and on report, June 13, have been incorporated, so that this synopsis represents the income tax provisions applicable to the current fiscal year.

Relief in respect of wife, children, and dependent relatives.—If his total income does not exceed £800 ($4,000), the taxpayer is entitled to relief from tax upon £25 ($125) in respect of (i) a wife living with him, or, in the case of a widower, any female relative, either of himself or of his deceased wife, who takes care of his children,[1] (ii) each child under 16 (including stepchildren and adopted children), and (iii) each dependent relative (incapacitated by old age or infirmity and whose income does not exceed £25 a year) whom he maintains.[1] On incomes from £800 to £1,000 ($4,000 to $5,000) relief from tax upon £25 is granted in respect of each child under 16 above the number of two.[1]

Relief in respect of life-insurance premiums, etc.—Relief from the normal tax is granted to the taxpayer on the amount of annual premiums for life insurance or deferred annuity on his own life or the life of his wife, but this allowance shall not reduce the income as estimated for purposes of exemption or abatement, neither shall it exceed one-sixth of the total income or 7 per cent of the capital sum insured or £100 ($500) in all. War-insurance premiums are not taken into account in calculating these limits.

REDUCTION OF RATE OF TAX.

Earned income relief.—Where the income does not exceed £2,500 ($12,500) and any part of that income is earned income, the following graduated rates instead of the normal tax are applicable to the earned income:

Where total earned and unearned income—	Rate on earned income— In the pound.	Per cent.
	s. d.	
Does not exceed £500 ($2,500)	2 3	11¼
Exceeds £500 ($2,500) and does not exceed £1,000 ($5,000)	3 0	15
Exceeds £1,000 ($5,000) and does not exceed £1,500 ($7,500)	3 9	18¾
Exceeds £1,500 ($7,500) and does not exceed £2,000 ($10,000)	4 6	22½
Exceeds £2,000 ($10,000) and does not exceed £2,500 ($12,500)	5 3	26¼

These rates are applied to the earned income after deducting from it the amount of income relieved of tax because of abatement on account of income not exceeding £700, or relief in respect of wife, children, or dependent relatives, or in respect of life insurance or deferred annuity premiums.

"Earned income" is defined to mean—

(i) Any income arising in respect of any remuneration from any office or employment of profit held by the individual, or in respect of any pension, superannuation, or other allowance, deferred pay, or compensation for loss of office, given in respect of the past services of the individual or of the husband or parent of the individual in any office or employment of profit, whether the individual or husband or parent of the individual shall have contributed to such pension, superannuation, allowance, or deferred pay or not; and

[1] Finance bill, 1918, as amended.

(ii) Any income from any property which is attached to or forms part of the emoluments of any office or employment of profit held by the individual; and

(iii) Any income which is charged under Schedule B or Schedule D, or the rules prescribed by Schedule D, and is immediately derived by the individual from the carrying on or exercise by him of his trade, profession, or vocation, either as an individual or, in the case of a partnership, as a partner personally acting therein.

Unearned income relief.—Where the income does not exceed £2,000 ($10,000), the following graduated rates, instead of the normal tax, are applicable to the unearned income:

Where total earned and unearned income—	Rate on unearned income—	
	In the pound.	Per cent.
	s. d.	
Does not exceed £500 ($2,500)	3 0	15
Exceeds £500 ($2,500) and does not exceed £1,000 ($5,000)	3 9	18¾
Exceeds £1,000 ($5,000) and does not exceed £1,500 ($7,500)	4 6	22½
Exceeds £1,500 ($7,500) and does not exceed £2,000 ($10,000)	5 3	26¼

SPECIAL WAR PROVISIONS.

Reduced rates on pay of soldiers, sailors, etc.—The service pay of any person in the army, navy, air service, or Red Cross (if stationed abroad), is taxed as follows:

If the person's total income—	Rate of tax—	
	In the pound.	Per cent.
	s. d.	
Does not exceed £300 ($1,500)	9	3¾
Exceeds £300 ($1,500) but does not exceed £500 ($2,500)	1 3	6¼
Exceeds £500 ($2,500) but does not exceed £1,000 ($5,000)	1 9	8¾
Exceeds £1,000 ($5,000) but does not exceed £1,500 ($7,500)	2 3	11¼
Exceeds £1,500 ($7,500) but does not exceed £2,000 ($10,000)	2 9	13¾
Exceeds £2,000 ($10,000) but does not exceed £2,500 ($12,500)	3 3	16¼
Exceeds £2,500 ($12,500)	3 6	17½

Abatement in case of soldiers, sailors, etc.—If the total income does not exceed £300 ($1,500), the prewar abatement of £160 ($800) is granted. Otherwise the new scale of allowances operates instead.

Diminution of profits owing to war.—When such person is assessed as to profits under Schedule D and can prove a diminution of income due to the war, he may recover the tax paid as to the amount of such diminution. Other persons suffering similar diminution of income taxable under that schedule may recover only in so far as the profits for the year are proved to have been less than the average profits of the last three years.

III. Classification of Income.

The properties, profits, and gains in this respect of which income tax is payable are classified under five schedules and the tax is imposed for every 20 shillings, or pound sterling, of the annual value·

Schedule A.—Property in all lands, tenements, hereditaments, and heritages in the United Kingdom.

Schedule B.—Occupation of all such lands, tenements, hereditaments, and heritages.

Schedule C.—All profits arising from interest, annuities, dividends, and shares of annuities payable to any person, body politic or corporate, company, or society, whether corporate or not, out of any public revenue.

Schedule D.—The annual profits or gains arising or accruing to any person residing in the United Kingdom from any kind of property whatever, whether situate in the United Kingdom or elsewhere, and the annual profits or gains arising or accruing to any person residing in the United Kingdom from any profession, trade, employment, or vocation, whether the same shall be respectively carried out in the United Kingdom or elsewhere.

And the annual profits or gains arising or accruing to any person whatever, and whether a subject of His Majesty or not, although not resident within the United Kingdom, from any profit whatever in the United Kingdom, or any profession, trade, employment, or vocation exercised within the United Kingdom.

And all interest of money, annuities, and other annual profits and gains not charged by virtue of any of the other schedules.

Schedule E.—Every public office or employment of profit, and upon every annuity, pension, or stipend payable by His Majesty, or out of the public revenues of the United Kingdom, except annuities charged to the duties under Schedule C.

IV. Application of the Schedules.

The following summary shows briefly the persons affected by the various schedules, how the tax is levied under such schedule, and the principal features of the elaborate system of rules for estimating the tax payable in respect of the several kinds of property:

SCHEDULE A.

[Landlord's property tax.]

The tax under this schedule affects all persons receiving rent or other annual payments or incomes from lands or houses. It is, with certain exceptions, levied on the occupier, and if he is a tenant he has the right of deducting any tax paid by him or a proportionate part thereof from his next payment of rent, thus throwing the burden of the tax on the landlord. Charge is made on the landlord directly in the case of houses renting for less than £10 a year, properties let for less than a year, and apartment or tenement houses. He may be charged directly in other cases if he files a written request to that effect before a specified date. The annual value of lands, buildings, etc., capable of actual occupation on which tax is imposed is the amount of the rent by the year for which they are or could be let.

Exemption may be granted in respect of public buildings and offices of universities and colleges, hospitals, almhouses, public schools, and literary and scientific institutions, and allowance made for amount expended on repairs of such buildings.

In the case of quarries, mines, iron works, gas works, salt or alum works, water works, canals and inland waterways, railways, toll roads, bridges, docks, ferries, etc., under this schedule, the tax is charged on the person or body of persons carrying on the concern and deducted from profits before they are distributed. The annual value on which the tax is imposed is defined to be the profits of the preceding year, except that in the case of coal or metalliferous mines an average of the five preceding years is taken.

SCHEDULE B.

[Farmer's tax.]

This is a tax on the occupation of those kinds of land of which the ownership is taxed under Schedule A. It affects principally the income of farmers, and since few farmers keep an accurate account of their profits, the annual taxable value is defined by law: formerly, by the law of 1896, as one-third the amount of the rent, and, by the law of 1915, as the full amount of the rent; for the future, according to the Finance bill of 1918, as double the amount of the rent.[1] Such rent does not include the rental of warehouses or buildings occupied for the carrying on of a trade or profession, nor of dwelling houses when these are rented with the farm for the purpose of farming.

The occupant has, however, if he is a farmer or a manager of woodlands on a commercial basis, the option of having his actual annual profits, computed according to the provisions of Schedule D, taken as the basis of the tax. In order to exercise this right, he must give written notice within a fixed time.

When an occupant engaged in farming only has incurred a loss, he is entitled, on giving notice within six months after the year of assessment, to recover so much of the tax as corresponds to the amount of the loss. Losses by flood or tempest because of which the tenant has received an abatement of rent from the landlord, or similar losses in the case of occupant owners, permit of a corresponding reduction of the amount of the tax.

The occupant, if a farmer, may pay the tax in two semiannual installments.

NOTE.—Where the land is occupied by the owner he is chargeable under both Schedule A and Schedule B.

SCHEDULE C.

[Tax on holders of British or foreign government securities.]

This includes all income, whether in the form of interest, annuities, dividends, or shares of annuities, arising out of any public revenue, British, colonial, or foreign. The amount of the tax is assessed at its source, before the taxable income reaches the taxpayer, upon the persons and corporations entrusted with the payment of such income. In this class are included all bankers or persons acting as bankers, who sell coupons for bills of exchange; all persons who by means of

---

[1] In the committee stage of the bill, June 3, 1918, an amendment was adopted providing that lands not occupied for the purposes of husbandry only, or mainly for those purposes (*e. g.*, recreation grounds, open spaces, etc.), should be assessed under this schedule on their annual value instead of on double the annual value. (106 H. C. deb. 1293.)

coupons obtain payments elsewhere than in the United Kingdom: dealers in coupons buying coupons for dividends otherwise than from a banker or other dealer.

Half-yearly payments of less than 50s. are exempt from the tax. Exemptions are also under certain circumstances granted, upon written request, to trade unions, friendly societies, savings banks, the Crown, ministers representing foreign nations, charitable trusts, trusts for keeping churches in repair.

Exempt from the tax under this schedule are the interest on the securities which represent subscriptions by any bank to any Government war loan; and the interest on securities issued under the war loan acts, 1914 to 1917, when the Treasury so directs. In the former case the interest is taxed under Schedule D, case 1, in the latter under Schedule D, case 3.

Taxable are dividends, etc., where the title is proved by any book or list ordinarily kept in the United Kingdom, except that no nonresident may be taxed on foreign or colonial securities.

No banker or other person may be compelled, under this schedule, to disclose the private affairs of any one on whose behalf he may be acting.

SCHEDULE D.

[Tax on business profits, professional incomes, and on sources of income not included under any other schedule.]

CASE 1. *Businesses, manufacturers, and concerns in the nature of a business, not contained in any other schedule.*—This case covers all resident persons or corporate bodies as to all enterprises carried on by them, whether at home or abroad, except such as fall under Schedule A.

Profits are computed without deduction for ordinary debts; for sums recoverable under an insurance or contract of indemnity; for what the capital employed in the business might have brought if put out at interest; for capital withdrawn from the business. On the other hand, deduction is allowed for debts proved to be bad debts; for repairs of premises; for supply, repairs or alteration of implements not exceeding the average amount so paid out during the preceding three years; for replacing machinery or plant (this deduction, however, to be diminished by the sum of any previous deductions on the same account together with amounts realized by the sale of the old machinery or plant); and, in the discretion of the tax commissioners, for not more than two-thirds the amount of the rental of the place of business, etc., provided that the premises are in the United Kingdom.

When a person carries on two or more enterprises and one or more of them results in a loss, such losses may be set off against the profits of the other enterprises.

Chargeable under this case are interest on securities representing a bank's subscription to the war loan; and income from investment of domestic life-insurance funds.

CASE 2. *Professions, employments, and vocations not contained in any other schedule.*

Provisions applicable both to Cases 1 and 2.—The basis of assessment under both these cases is the average income for the three trade years preceding the assessment, except that weekly wage earners employed at manual labor are assessed for the quarter instead of for the year.

No deductions are allowed for money not exclusively spent in pursuance of the business or profession; for the maintenance of the taxpayer, his family, or his establishment; for the rental of any portion of office or dwelling house not used for the purpose of the business or profession: for the rental of a place of business outside the United Kingdom.

On the other hand, deduction is allowable for payment of excess profits duty and munitions exchequer payments and for depreciation, provided, in the latter case, that it may not, when added to sums allowed for depreciation during any previous year, exceed the total value of the plant or machinery.

Profits from lands are not included under either of these cases. The profits of a partnership are considered as a unit, and are considered independently of any other business or profession in which any of the partners is engaged. (This is the only exception to the principle that each person is charged upon the aggregate of all those of his enterprises which come under Schedule D.) A change in the personnel of a partnership does not affect the assessment, unless it can be proved that the change resulted in or was followed by a diminution of the profits.

CASE 3. *Income of an uncertain annual value not charged under Schedule A.*—Under this case are chargeable income from all securities bearing interest payable out of the public revenue and not charged under Schedule C; income from all discounts and all interest not annual: interest from such war loans as are issued with the provision that they be not subject to deduction of the income tax (at the source); investment income of foreign and colonial insurance companies: profits of dealers in cattle or milk beyond such as are computed under Schedule B, when the land occupied by the dealers is not sufficient for the keep of the cattle and the rental of such land is found to be an insufficient indication of the profits.

The minimum taxable income under this case is that arising from the same source during the preceding year.

CASE 4. *Income from foreign and colonial securities.*—Exempt from taxation under this case is interest taxable under Schedule C, and, in the case of a taxpayer not permanently a resident of the United Kingdom, such interest as is not actually received by him there during the assessment year. Residents, on the other hand, are liable for interest even when it is not received by them in the United Kingdom.

The income received from the same source during the preceding year is taken as the basis of assessment, and deduction is allowed when such income is subject to the payment of annual interest or annuity to a nonresident. Neither in this case nor in case 5, however, is deduction allowed for expenses of distribution.

CASE 5. *Income from foreign and colonial possessions.*—Taxable under this case are, in the case of a resident, the income from stocks, shares, or rents, whether or not received in the United Kingdom; in the case of a nonresident, the income from stocks, shares, or rents only in so far as it is received in the United Kingdom; in the case of either, income from other property, only in so far as received in the United Kingdom.

The assessment is on the basis of the average of the three preceding trade years.

CASE 6. *Annual income not falling under any other case or schedule.*—To be computed upon full information given to the authorities, on whatever time basis they find proper.

Provisions applicable to all cases under Schedule D.—If a business or professional firm, etc., ceases altogether, through death, bankruptcy, or for any other cause, an amendment of the assessment may be applied for within a fixed time after the assessment year.

If the owner or incumbent is succeeded by another person, the assessment continues to hold good, unless cause to the contrary be shown. If such succession occurs during an assessment year, the portion which each party is to pay is determined by the tax officials, who are authorized to make the necessary refunds.

In the case of interests, annuities, and other annual payments made out of the income from lands, heritages, offices, or employments, annuities, pensions, stipends or shares of public annuities, the tax is correspondingly reduced. In the case of annual payments made out of other sources of income, the reduction is at the discretion of the tax authorities.

Income is held to arise in the United Kingdom and to be taxable under this act when its source is a business, profession, etc., which is either carried on there, or which has its center of management there, wherever carried on. Where control of a business is situated abroad, such business shall be held to be foreign and so assessed on its operations within the United Kingdom, even though some of its partners are residents.

The incomes of charitable trusts, of certain friendly societies, and of certain trade unions are exempt from taxation under this schedule.

SCHEDULE E.

[Tax on the salaries of public officials and employees.]

Taxable under this section, in addition to all civil and military officials and employees of the Crown, are offices or employments under any ecclesiastical body, under any public institution or foundation of whatever nature, under any public corporation or local authority, and under any trustees of public funds, tolls, or duties; as well as all other public offices and all other employments of a public nature. Taxable under this schedule, also, as a result of a somewhat strained interpretation embodied in the Companies Act of the phrase in the original act of 1842, "offices or employments of profit under any company or society, whether corporate or noncorporate," are the officials of limited-liability companies. This has occasioned considerable difficulty, since the basis of assessment under this schedule is the annual salary, rather than the average salary, as under Schedule D.

The income taxable under this schedule is not merely that received in payment of current services, but also all annuities, pensions, stipends, including voluntary grants, and even Easter offerings made to clergymen by their congregations. Allowances are, however, made in certain cases for expenses connected with the office or employment.

Wage earners employed at manual labor do not come under this schedule. And certain classes of persons who come under the schedule if publicly employed, are held not to come under it if employed by limited-liability companies. Such is the case with subordinate employees, and with persons whose head office is in the United Kingdom but who are employed abroad.

List of Income-Tax Acts in Force

1842. Income-tax act, 1842 (5 and 6 Vict., c. 35), secs. 3–24, 28–36, 38–81, 83–86, 88–89, 93–103, 105–106, 110–142, 146–147, 149–151, 153–156, 158–174, 176–180, 182–191.
Land-tax act, 1842 (5 and 6 Vict., c. 37), secs. 3–5.
Income-tax (foreign dividends) act, 1842 (5 and 6 Vict., c 80), sec. 2.
1853. Income-tax act, 1853 (16 and 17 Vict., c. 34), secs. 2–26, 29–32, 34–41, 43, 47–56, 58.
Income-tax (insurance) act, 1853 (16 and 17 Vict., c 91), sec. 1.
1854. Income-tax act, 1854 (17 and 18 Vict, c. 24), sec. 5.
1855. Income-tax (insurance) act, 1855 (18 and 19 Vict., c. 35), sec. 1
1856. Taxes act, 1856 (19 and 20 Vict., c. 80), sec. 1.
1859. Income-tax act, 1859 (22 and 23 Vict., c 18), sec 6
1860. Income-tax act, 1860 (23 and 24 Vict., c 14), secs. 4–7, 10.
1861. Revenue (No 2) act, 1861 (24 and 25 Vict., c. 91), sec. 36.
1863. Revenue act, 1863 (26 and 27 Vict., c 33), sec. 22.
1864. Revenue (No. 1) act, 1864 (27 and 28 Vict., c. 18), sec. 15.
1865. Revenue act, 1865 (28 and 29 Vict., c. 30), sec. 6
1866. Revenue act, 1866 (29 and 30 Vict., c. 36), secs. 8–9.
1868. Revenue act, 1868 (31 and 32 Vict, c. 28), sec. 5
1872. Income-tax (public offices) act, 1872 (35 and 36 Vict, c. 82), sec 1 (1).
1878. Customs and inland revenue act, 1878 (41 and 42 Vict., c. 15), secs. 12, 16
1879. Customs and inland revenue act. 1879 (42 and 43 Vict., c. 21), sec. 18.
1880. Taxes management act, 1880 (43 and 44 Vict., c. 19), secs. 5, 8 (2), 10, 13, 15–19, 20 (7–8), 21–24, 26–37, 39–46, 48–61 (1), 62–70, 72–79, 81–97, 101–103, 105–106, 108–113, 115, 116 (1), 117–121, schedule 2.
1881. Customs and inland revenue act, 1881 (44 and 45 Vict. c. 12), sec 23.
1883. Revenue act, 1883 (46 and 47 Vict., c. 55), sec. 12.
1884. Revenue act, 1884 (47 and 48 Vict., c. 62), secs. 6–7.
1885. Customs and inland revenue act, 1885 (48 and 49 Vict., c. 51), secs. 25–26.
1887. Customs and inland revenue act, 1887 (50 and 51 Vict., c. 15), sec. 18.
1888. Customs and inland revenue act, 1888 (51 and 52 Vict., c. 8), sec 24.
1889. Revenue act, 1889 (52 and 53 Vict., c. 42), secs. 10, 12–14.
1890. Customs and inland revenue act, 1890 (53 and 54 Vict, c. 8), secs. 23–24, 27–28, 30
Inland revenue regulation act, 1890 (53 and 54 Vict., c 21), secs. 1, 4 (1)–(3), 8, 11, 21 (1), 22, 29 (2), 33 (2), 35–36
1891. Taxes (regulation of remuneration) act, 1891 (54 and 55 Vict, c. 13), secs. 1–6.
1892. Taxes (regulation of remuneration) amendment act, 1892 (55 and 56 Vict., c. 25), sec. 1 (2).
1893. Trades-union (provident funds) act, 1893 (56 and 57 Vict., c 2), secs. 1–3.
Customs and inland revenue act, 1893 (56 and 57 Vict., c. 7), sec. 7.
Industrial and provident societies act, 1893 (56 and 57 Vict., c. 39), sec. 24.
1894. Finance act, 1894 (57 and 58 Vict, c. 30), secs, 34 (1), 35, 36.
1896. Finance act, 1896 (59 and 60 Vict., c. 28), secs. 26–28, 30.
1897. Finance act, 1897 (60 and 61 Vict., c. 24), sec. 5
1898. Finance act, 1898 (61 and 62 Vict., c 10), secs. 8–10, 16.
1903. Revenue act, 1903 (3 Edw. 7, c. 46), secs. 10, 12, 13.
1904. Finance act, 1904 (4 Edw. 7, c. 7), secs. 8–9.
1906. Revenue act, 1906 (6 Edw. 7, c. 20), sec. 11.
1907. Finance act, 1907 (7 Edw. 7, c. 13), secs 19–23, 24 (2)–28.
1908. Finance act, 1908 (8 Edw 7, c. 16), sec. 8.
1910. Finance (1909–10) act, 1910 (10 Edw. 7, c. 8), secs 66, 68–72, 93, 94.
1911. Revenue act, 1911 (1 Geo. 5, c. 2), secs. 12–14.
1912. Finance act, 1912 (2 and 3 Geo. 5, c. 8), secs. 6–7.
1913. Finance act, 1913 (3 and 4 Geo 5, c. 30), sec. 3.
1914. Finance act, 1914 (4 and 5 Geo. 5, c. 10), secs. 4–5, 7–9 (3), 10, 11.
Finance act, 1914 (session 2) (5 Geo. 5, c. 7), sec. 13.
1915. Finance act, 1915 (5 and 6 Geo. 5, c. 62), secs. 11–23, 28 (1).
Finance (No. 2) act, 1915 (5 and 6 Geo. 5, c. 89), secs. 21–22, 24, 26–36, 47, 50.
War loan (supplemental provisions) act, 1915 (5 and 6 Geo. 5, c. 93), sec. 3.
1916. Finance act, 1916 (6 and 7 Geo. 5, c. 24), secs. 25–33, 35–40, 42–44, 48 (2), 53, 57, 63, 64.
1917. Finance act, 1917 (7 and 8 Geo 5, c. 31), secs. 11–19.

68422—18——2

BILLS

1918. Income-tax bill [H L.] (1) introduced in the House of Lords February 19, 1918, to consolidate the laws in force August, 1917.

Finance bill, 1918 [Bill 24], clauses 19–33, 39, introduced in the House of Commons May 1, 1918, amendments to clauses 23, 26, 28, adopted in committee of the whole June 3 (106 H C. Deb. 1293, 1346), and on report June 13.

NOTE.—The House of Lords bill, 1918 (1), to consolidate the enactments relating to income tax, is the most convenient text of the law in force in systematic order. For ready reference on a particular topic the most useful manuals are W. E. Snelling's "Income-tax and supertax law and cases," third edition, and "Income-tax and supertax practice," second edition (London, Sir Isaac Pitman & Sons, 1918), in which the statute and case law and its application to current business practice, respectively, are arranged under subject-headings, in alphabetical order. The author of these works is an official of the Inland Revenue Department, experienced in the administration of the income-tax acts.

TABLE SHOWING AMOUNT OF TAX PAYABLE ON CERTAIN INCOMES AND EFFECTIVE RATE CHARGED UNDER THE BUDGET PROPOSALS OF 1918.

(a) Income tax.

Income.	Wholly earned.		Wholly unearned		Income.	Wholly earned		Wholly unearned.	
	Amount of tax.	Effective rate.	Amount of tax	Effective rate.		Amount of tax	Effective rate.	Amount of tax.	Effective rate
£	£ s. d.	s. d.	£ s d	s. d			Per cent		Per cent
131.	1 0 0	0 2	1 0 0	0 2	$655	$5 00	76	$5 00	76
150.	3 7 6	0 5	4 10 0	0 7	750	16 87	2 24	22 50	3
200.	9 0 0	0 11	12 0 0	1 2	1,000	45 00	4 5	60.00	6
250.	14 12 6	1 2	19 10 0	1 7	1,250	73 12	5 85	97.50	7.8
300.	20 5 0	1 4	27 0 0	1 10	1,500	101 25	6.76	135 00	9
350.	25 17 6	1 6	34 10 0	2 0	1,750	129 37	7 39	172 50	9 86
400.	31 10 0	1 7	42 0 0	2 1	2,000	157 50	7.87	210 00	10 5
450.	39 7 6	1 9	52 10 0	2 4	2,250	196 87	8.75	262 50	11 67
500.	45 0 0	1 10	60 0 0	2 5	2,500	225 00	9	300.00	12
550.	67 10 0	2 5	84 7 6	3 1	2,750	337 50	12 27	421 87	15 34
600.	75 0 0	2 6	93 15 0	3 1	3,000	375 00	12 5	468 75	15 62
650.	87 0 0	2 8	108 15 0	3 4	3,250	435 00	13.38	543 75	16.73
700.	94 10 0	2 8	118 2 6	3 4	3,500	472 50	13.5	590 62	16 87
800.	120 0 0	3 0	150 0 0	3 9	4,000	600 00	15	750 00	18.75
900.	135 0 0	3 0	168 15 0	3 9	4,500	675 00	15	843 75	18 75
1,000.	150 0 0	3 0	187 10 0	3 9	5,000	750 00	15	937 50	18 75
1,500.	281 5 0	3 9	337 10 0	4 6	7,500	1,406 25	18 75	1,687 50	22 5
2,000.	450 0 0	4 6	525 0 0	5 3	10,000	2,250 00	22.5	2,625 00	26 25
2,500.	656 5 0	5 3	750 0 0	6 0	12,500	3,281 25	26 25	3,750 00	30

(b) Income tax and supertax.

Income.	Income tax.	Supertax.	Total tax.	Effective rate.	Income.	Income tax.	Super-tax	Total tax.	Effective rate
£	£	£ s.	£ s.	s. d					Per ct.
2,750	825	43 15	868 15	6 4	$13,750	$4,125	$218.75	$4,343.75	31.59
3,000	900	62 10	962 10	6 5	15,000	4,500	312.50	4,812 50	32.08
4,000	1,200	162 10	1,362 10	6 10	20,000	6,000	812.50	6,812.50	34 16
5,000	1,500	287 10	1,787 10	7 2	25,000	7,500	1,437.50	8,937.50	35.75
6,000	1,800	437 10	2,237 10	7 5	30,000	9,000	2,187.50	11,187.50	37.29
7,000	2,100	612 10	2,712 10	7 9	35,000	10,500	3,062.50	13,562.50	38.75
8,000	2,400	787 10	3,187 10	8 0	40,000	12,000	3,937.50	15,937 50	39.84
9,000	2,700	987 10	3,687 10	8 2	45,000	13,500	4,937.50	18,437 50	40.97
10,000	3,000	1,187 10	4,187 10	8 4	50,000	15,000	5,937.50	20,937.50	41.87
11,000	3,300	1,412 10	4,712 10	8 7	55,000	16,500	7,062.50	23,562.50	42.84
12,000	3,600	1,637 10	5,237 10	8 9	60,000	18,000	8,187.50	26,187 50	43 65
13,000	3,900	1,862 10	5,762 10	8 10	65,000	19.500	9,312.50	28,812.50	44.33
14,000	4,200	2,087 10	6,287 10	9 0	70,000	21,000	10,437.50	31,437 50	44.91
15,000	4,500	2,312 10	6,812 10	9 1	75,000	22,500	11,562.50	34,062 50	45.42
20,000	6,000	3,437 10	9,437 10	9 5	100,000	30,000	17,187.50	47,187 50	47.18
25,000	7,500	4,562 10	12,062 10	9 8	125,000	37,500	22,812.50	60,312 50	48.25
30,000	9,000	5,687 10	14,687 10	9 9	150,000	45,000	28,437.50	73,437.50	48.96
40,000	12,000	7,937 10	19,937 10	10 0	200,000	60,000	39,687.50	99,687.50	49.84
50,000	15,000	10,187 10	25,187 10	10 1	250,000	75,000	50,937 50	125,937.50	50.37
100,000	30,000	21,437 10	51,437 10	10 3	500,000	150,000	107,187.50	257,187.50	51.44
150,000	45,000	32,687 10	77,687 10	10 4	750,000	225,000	163,437.50	388,437.50	51.79
200,000	60,000	43,937 10	103,937 10	10 5	1,000,000	300,000	219,687.50	519,687.50	51.97

CANADA.

INCOME WAR TAX ACT, 1917.

[7 and 8 Geo. V, c 28, as amended in 1918.]

AN ACT TO AUTHORIZE THE LEVYING OF A WAR TAX UPON CERTAIN INCOMES.

[Assented to 20th September, 1917.]

His Majesty, by and with the advice and consent of the Senate and House of Commons of Canada, enacts as follows:

1. This act may be cited as the Income War Tax Act, 1917.

DEFINITIONS.

2. In this act, and in any regulations made under this act, unless the context otherwise requires—

(*a*) "Board" means a Board of Referees appointed under section 12 hereof.

(*b*) "Minister" means the Minister of Finance.

(*c*) "Normal tax" means the tax authorized by paragraph (*a*) of section 4 of this act.

(*d*) "Person" means any individual or person and any syndicate, trust, association, or other body and any body corporate, and the heirs, executors, administrators, curators, and assigns, or other legal representatives of such person, according to the law of that part of Canada to which the context extends.

(*e*) "Supertax" means the taxes authorized by paragraphs (*b*) to (*m*), both inclusive, of section 4 of this act.

(*f*) "Taxpayer" means any person paying, liable to pay, or believed by the minister to be liable to pay, any tax imposed by this act.

(*g*) "Year" means the calendar year.

(*h*) "Surtax" means the taxes authorized by paragraphs (*n*) to (*q*), both inclusive, of section 4 of this act.

(*i*) "Dependent child" means a child under 21 years of age and dependent on his parent for support, or over 21 years of age and dependent on his parent for support on account of physical or mental incapacity.

INCOME.

3. (1) For the purposes of this act, "income" means the annual net profit or gain or gratuity, whether ascertained and capable of computation as being wages, salary, or other fixed amount, or unascertained as being fees or emoluments, or as being profits from a trade or commercial or financial or other business or calling, directly or indirectly received by a person from any office or employment, or

from any profession or calling, or from any trade, manufacture, or business, as the case may be, and shall include the interest, dividends, or profits directly or indirectly received from money at interest upon any security or without security, or from stocks, or from any other investment, and, whether such gains or profits are divided or distributed or not, and also the annual profit or gain from any other source, including the income from but not the value of property acquired by gift, bequest, devise, or descent; and including the income from but not the proceeds of life insurance policies paid upon the death of the person insured, or payments made or credited to the insured on life insurance endowment or annuity contracts upon the maturity of the term mentioned in the contract or upon the surrender of the contract; with the following exemptions and deductions:

EXEMPTIONS AND DEDUCTIONS.

(*a*) Such reasonable allowance as may be allowed by the minister for depreciation, or for any expenditure of a capital nature for renewals, or for the development of a business, and the minister, when determining the income derived from mining and from oil and gas wells, shall make an allowance for the exhaustion of the mines and wells.

(*b*) $200 for each child under 16 years of age who is dependent upon the taxpayer for support.

(*c*) Amounts paid by the taxpayer during the year to the Patriotic and Canadian Red Cross funds, and other patriotic and war funds approved by the minister.

(*d*) For the purposes of the normal tax, the income embraced in a personal return shall be credited with the amount received as dividends upon the stock of any company or other person which is taxable upon its income under this act: *Provided, however,* That in determining the income the personal and living expenses shall not be taken into consideration.

HOLDING COMPANIES.

(2) Where an incorporated company conducts its business, whether under agreement or otherwise, in such manner as either directly or indirectly to benefit its shareholders or any of them, or any persons directly or indirectly interested in such company, by selling its product or the goods and commodities in which it deals at less than the fair price which might be obtained therefor, the minister may, for the purposes of this act, determine the amount which shall be deemed to be the income of such company for the year, and in determining such amount the minister shall have regard to the fair price which, but for any agreement, arrangement, or understanding, might be or could have been obtained for such product, goods, and commodities.

NONRESIDENTS.

(3) In the case of the income of persons residing or having their head office or principal place of business outside of Canada but carrying on business in Canada, either directly or through or in the name of any other person, the income shall be the net profit or gain arising from the business of such person in Canada.

UNDISTRIBUTED GAINS.

(4) For the purpose of the supertax only, the income of a taxpayer shall include the share to which he would be entitled of the undivided or undistributed gains and profits made by any syndicate, trust, association, corporation, or other body, or any partnership, if such gains and profits were divided or distributed, unless the minister is of opinion that the accumulation of such undivided and undistributed gains and profits is not made for the purpose of evading the tax, and is not in excess of what is reasonably required for the purposes of the business.

INCOME TAX.

4. (1) There shall be assessed, levied and paid upon the income during the preceding year of every person residing or ordinarily resident in Canada or carrying on any business in Canada, and upon the income received by any person from any source within Canada, the following taxes:

(*a*) Two per centum upon all income exceeding $1,000 but not exceeding $1,500, in the case of unmarried persons and widows or widowers without dependent children, and exceeding $2,000 but not exceeding $3,000, in the case of all other persons; 4 per centum upon all income exceeding $1,500, in the case of unmarried persons and widows or widowers without dependent children, and exceeding $3,000 in the case of all other persons.

SUPERTAX.

And in addition thereto the following supertax:

(*b*) Two per centum upon the amount by which the income exceeds $6,000 and does not exceed $10,000.

(*c*) Five per centum upon the amount by which the income exceeds $10,000 and does not exceed $20,000.

(*d*) Eight per centum of the amount by which the income exceeds $20,000 and does not exceed $30,000.

(*e*) Ten per centum of the amount by which the income exceeds $30,000 and does not exceed $50,000.

(*f*) Fifteen per centum of the amount by which the income exceeds $50,000 and does not exceed $75,000.

(*g*) Twenty per centum of the amount by which the income exceeds $75,000 and does not exceed $100,000.

(*h*) Twenty-five per centum of the amount by which the income exceeds $100,000 and does not exceed $200,000.

(*i*) Thirty per centum of the amount by which the income exceeds $200,000 and does not exceed $400,000.

(*j*) Thirty-five per centum of the amount by which the income exceeds $400,000 and does not exceed $600,000.

(*k*) Forty per centum of the amount by which the income exceeds $600,000 and does not exceed $800,000.

(*l*) Forty-five per centum of the amount by which the income exceeds $800,000 and does not exceed $1,000,000.

(*m*) Fifty per centum of the amount by which the income exceeds $1,000,000.

SURTAX.

And in addition thereto the following surtax:

(*n*) Upon income in excess of $6,000 but not exceeding $10,000, 5 per cent of the normal tax and supertax payable thereon.

(*o*) Upon income in excess of $10,000 but not exceeding $100,000, 10 per cent of the normal tax and supertax payable thereon.

(*p*) Upon income exceeding $100,000 but not exceeding $200,000, 15 per cent of the normal tax and supertax payable thereon.

(*q*) Upon income exceeding $200,000, 35 per cent of the normal tax and supertax payable thereon.

CORPORATION INCOME TAX.

(2) Corporations and joint-stock companies, no matter how created or organized, shall pay 6 per cent upon income exceeding $3,000, but shall not be liable to pay the supertax or surtax; and the minister may permit any corporation or joint-stock company the fiscal year of which is not the calendar year, to make a return and to have the tax payable by it computed upon its income for the 12 months ending with its last fiscal year preceding the date of assessment.

PARTNERSHIPS NOT LIABLE TO TAX.

(3) Any persons carrying on business in partnership shall be liable for the income tax only in their individual capacity.

TRANSFER OF PROPERTY TO EVADE TAXATION.

(4) A person who, after the 1st day of August, 1917, has reduced his income by the transfer or assignment of any real or personal movable or immovable property, to such person's wife or husband, as the case may be, or to any member of the family of such person, shall, nevertheless, be liable to be taxed as if such transfer or assignment had not been made, unless the minister is satisfied that such transfer or assignment was not made for the purpose of evading the taxes imposed under this act or any part thereof.

DEDUCTIONS ALLOWED—WAR TAXES.

(5) Taxpayers shall be entitled to the following deductions from the amounts that would otherwise be payable by them for income tax—

(*a*) From the income tax accruing for the year 1917 the amounts paid by any taxpayer for taxes accruing during the year 1917 under the provisions of Part I of the Special War Revenue Act, 1915, and from the income tax payable for any year thereafter the amounts paid by the taxpayer for taxes accruing during such year under the said Part I of the said act.

(*b*) From the income tax accruing for the year 1917 the amounts paid by any taxpayer under the Business Profits War Tax Act, 1916, and any amendments thereto for any accounting period ending in the year 1917. In the case of a partnership each partner shall be entitled to deduct such portion of the tax paid by the partnership under the Business Profits War Tax Act, 1916, as may correspond to his interest in the income of the partnership.

INCOMES NOT LIABLE TO TAX.

5. The following incomes shall not be liable to taxation hereunder—

(*a*) The income of the Governor General of Canada.

(*b*) The incomes of consuls and consuls general who are citizens of the country they represent and who are not engaged in any other business or profession.

(*c*) The income of any company, commission, or association not less than 90 per cent of the stock or capital of which is owned by a Province or a municipality.

(*d*) The income of any religious, charitable, agricultural, and educational institutions, boards of trade, and chambers of commerce.

(*e*) The incomes of labor organizations and societies and of benevolent and fraternal beneficiary societies and orders.

(*f*) The incomes of mutual corporations not having a capital represented by shares, no part of the income of which inures to the profit of any member thereof, and of life insurance companies except such amount as is credited to shareholders' account.

(*g*) The incomes of clubs, societies, and associations organized and operated solely for social welfare, civic improvement, pleasure, recreation, or other nonprofitable purposes, no part of the income of which inures to the benefit of any stockholder or member.

(*h*) The incomes of such insurance, mortgage, and loan associations operated entirely for the benefit of farmers as are approved by the minister.

(*i*) The income derived from any bonds or other securities of the Dominion of Canada issued exempt from any income tax imposed in pursuance of any legislation enacted by the Parliament of Canada.

(*j*) The military and naval pay of persons who have been on active service overseas during the present war in any of the military or naval forces of His Majesty or any of His Majesty's allies.

(*k*) The income of incorporated companies whose business and assets are carried on and situate entirely outside of Canada.

6. [Repealed.]

ANNUAL RETURN OF TOTAL INCOME.

7. (1) Every person liable to taxation under this act shall, on or before the 28th day of February in each year, without any notice or demand, deliver to the minister a return, in such form as the minister may prescribe, of his total income during the last preceding calendar year. In such return the taxpayer shall state an address in Canada to which all notices and other documents to be mailed or served under this act may be mailed or sent.

RETURNS OF CORPORATIONS, ETC.

(2) The return in the case of a corporation, association, or other body shall be made and signed by the president, secretary, treasurer, or chief agent having a personal knowledge of the affairs of such

corporation, association, or other body, or, in any case, by such other person or persons employed in the business liable or believed to be liable to taxation, as the minister may require.

RETURN BY GUARDIAN, LEGAL REPRESENTATIVE, ETC.

(3) If a person liable to taxation hereunder is unable for any reason to make the return required by this section, such return shall be made by the guardian, curator, tutor, or other legal representative of such person, or, if there is no such legal representative, by some one acting as agent for such person, and in the case of the estate of any deceased person, by the executor, administrator, or heir of such deceased person, and if there is no person to make a return under the provisions of this subsection, then such person as may be required by the minister to make such return.

RETURNS BY EMPLOYERS OF SALARIES AND BY COMPANIES OF DIVIDENDS, ETC.

(4) All employers shall make a return of all persons in their employ receiving any salary or other remuneration, any portion of which is liable to taxation under this act, and all corporations, associations, and syndicates shall make a return of all dividends and bonuses paid to shareholders and members and all persons in whatever capacity acting, having the control, receipt, disposal, or payment of fixed or determinable annual or periodical gains, profits, or income of any taxpayer, shall make and render a separate and distinct return to the minister of such gains, profits, or income, containing the name and address of each taxpayer. Such returns shall be delivered to the minister on or before the 28th day of February in each year, without any notice or demand being made therefor, and in such form as the minister may prescribe.

(5) The minister may at any time enlarge the time for making any return.

ADDITIONAL INFORMATION.

8. (1) If the minister, in order to enable him to make an assessment, desires further information, or if he suspects that any person who has not made a return is liable to taxation hereunder, he may, by registered letter, require additional information, or a return containing such information as he deems necessary, to be furnished him within 30 days.

PRODUCTION OF LETTERS, ACCOUNTS, ETC.

(2) The minister may require the production, or the production on oath, by the taxpayer or by his agent or officer, or by any person or partnership holding, or paying, or liable to pay, any portion of the income of any taxpayer, of any letters, accounts, invoices, statements, and other documents.

INQUIRY AS TO INCOME.

(3) Any officer authorized thereto by the minister may make such inquiry as he may deem necessary for ascertaining the income of any taxpayer, and for the purposes of such inquiry such officer shall have all the powers and authority of a commissioner appointed under Part I of the Inquiries Act, Revised Statutes of Canada, 1906, chapter 104.

PENALTY.

9. (1) For every default in complying with the provisions of the two next preceding sections, the taxpayer, and also the person or persons required to make a return, shall each be liable on summary conviction to a penalty of $100 for each day during which the default continues.

(2) Any person making a false statement in any return or in any information required by the minister shall be liable on summary conviction to a penalty not exceeding $10,000 or to six months' imprisonment, or to both fine and imprisonment.

ASSESSMENT AND PAYMENT.

10. (1) The minister shall, on or before the 30th day of April in each year, or on or before such other date as he may in any case or cases prescribe, determine the several amounts payable for the tax, and shall thereupon send by registered mail a notice of assessment in such form as the minister may prescribe to each taxpayer, notifying him of the amount payable by him for the tax. The tax shall be paid within one month from the date of mailing of the notice of assessment. In default of payment, interest at the rate of 7 per cent per annum shall be paid on such tax until the said tax and interest are paid.

(2) The minister shall not be bound by any return or information supplied by or on behalf of a taxpayer, and notwithstanding such return or information, or if no return has been made, the minister may determine the amount of the tax to be paid by any person.

(3) Any person liable to pay the tax shall continue to be liable, and in case any person so liable shall fail to make a return as required by this act or shall make an incorrect or false return, and does not pay the tax in whole or in part, the minister may at any time assess such person for the tax, or such portion thereof as he may be liable to pay, and may prescribe the time within which any appeals may be made under the provisions of this act from the assessment or from the decision of the board and may fix the date of payment of the tax.

SECRECY.

11. No person employed in the service of His Majesty shall communicate or allow to be communicated to any person not legally entitled thereto any information obtained under the provisions of this act, or allow any such person to inspect or have access to any written statement furnished under the provisions of this act. Any person violating any of the provisions of this section shall be liable on summary conviction to a penalty not exceeding $200.

BOARD OF REFEREES.

12. (1) The governor in council may appoint a board or boards of referees, and may prescribe the territory or district within which a board shall exercise jurisdiction. A board shall consist of not more than three members, and the members of a board shall jointly and severally have all the powers and authority of a commissioner appointed under Part I of the Inquiries Act, Revised Statutes of Canada, 1906, chapter 104.

(2) Every member of the board shall take an oath of office in Form I of the schedule to this act before performing any duty under this act. All affidavits made in pursuance of this subsection shall be filed with the minister.

COURT OF REVISION.

13. A board shall act as a court of revision, and shall hear and determine any appeal made by a taxpayer under this act in such place in Canada as the minister may direct.

NOTICE OF APPEAL.

14. Any person objecting to the amount at which he is assessed, or as having been wrongfully assessed, may, personally or by his agent, within 20 days after the date of mailing of the notice of assessment, as provided in section 10 of this act, give notice in writing to the minister in Form II of the schedule to this act that he consider himself aggrieved for either of the causes aforesaid; otherwise such person's right to appeal shall cease, and the assessment made shall stand and be valid and binding upon all parties concerned, notwithstanding any defect, error, or omission that may have been made therein, or in any proceeding required by this act or any regulation hereunder; provided, however, that the minister, either before or after the expiry of the said 20 days, may give a taxpayer further time in which to appeal.

HEARING AND DECISION BY BOARD.

15. (1) A board, after hearing any evidence adduced, and upon such other inquiry as it considers advisable, shall determine the matter and confirm or amend the assessment accordingly. A board may increase the assessment in any case before it. The board shall send a copy of its decision by registered mail to the taxpayer or his agent or officer.

COSTS.

(2) In any case where the appeal is unsuccessful, the board may direct that the person who appealed shall pay the costs or part of the costs of such appeal; and if such appeal is successful, a board may recommend that the costs or any part thereof be paid by the Crown. The tariff of fees shall be as prescribed by the board.

PROCEEDING EX PARTE.

16. If the taxpayer fails to appear, either in person or by agent, the board may proceed ex parte or may defer the hearing.

APPEAL TO EXCHEQUER COURT.

17. If the taxpayer is dissatisfied with the decision of a board, he may, within 20 days after the mailing of the decision, give a written notice to the minister in Form III of the schedule to this act that he desires to appeal from such decision. If the taxpayer gives such notice, or if the minister is dissatisfied with the decision, the minister shall refer the matter to the Exchequer Court of Canada for hearing and determination, and such reference may be made in Form IV of the schedule to this act, and he shall notify the taxpayer by registered letter that he has made such reference. On any such reference the court shall hear and consider such matter upon the papers and evidence referred, and upon any further evidence which the taxpayer or the Crown produces under the direction of the court, and the decision of the Exchequer Court thereon shall be final and conclusive.

EXCLUSIVE JURISDICTION OF EXCHEQUER COURT.

18. Except as hereinafter expressly provided, the Exchequer Court shall have exclusive jurisdiction to hear and determine all questions that may arise in connection with any proceeding taken under this act and may award costs in connection therewith.

NO ASSESSMENT TO BE SET ASIDE FOR TECHNICAL REASONS.

19. (1) No assessment shall be set aside by a board or by the court upon the ground that there has been any error or omission in connection with any proceedings required to be taken under this act or any regulation hereunder, but such board or court in any case that may come before it may determine the true and proper amount of the tax to be paid hereunder.

PROCEEDINGS IN CAMERA.

(2) All the proceedings of the board and of the Exchequer Court shall be held in camera if requested by the taxpayer.

TAX A DEBT DUE THE CROWN.

20. The taxes and all interest and costs assessed or imposed under the provisions of this act shall be recoverable as a debt due to His Majesty from the person on whom it is assessed or imposed.

RECOVERY OF TAX, ETC.

21. Any tax, interest, costs, or penalty that may be assessed, recovered, or imposed under this act may, at the option of the minister, be recovered and imposed in the Exchequer Court of Canada or in any other court of competent jurisdiction in the name of His Majesty

MINISTER TO ADMINISTER ACT—REGULATIONS.

22. The minister shall have the administration of this act and the control and management of the collection of the taxation levied hereby and of all matters incident thereto, and of the officers and persons employed in that service. The minister may make any regulations deemed necessary for carrying this act into effect.

APPOINTMENT OF OFFICERS TO ADMINISTER ACT, AND THEIR SALARIES.

23. The governor in council may from time to time appoint officers and other persons to carry out this act or any order in council or regulations made thereunder, and the governor in council may assign the names of office of such officers and other persons, and grant such salaries or pay for their services and responsibilities as he deems necessary and reasonable, and may appoint the times and manner in which the same shall be paid.

FIRST RETURN UNDER ACT, FEBRUARY 28, 1918, AND 1917 FIRST YEAR'S INCOME TO BE TAXED.

24. The first return to be made by taxpayers under section 7 of this act shall be made on or before the 28th day of February, 1918, and all taxpayers shall (subject to the provisions of subsection 2 of section 4) be liable to taxation in respect of their income for the year ending the 31st day of December, 1917, and for each year thereafter, as provided by this act.

(Schedule of forms omitted.)

Comparative table of rates in Great Britain, Canada and United States on portions of income over $5,000.

Portion of income	Great Britain, 1918			Canada, 1918.				United States, 1917			
	Normal tax	Super-tax	Total per cent	Normal tax.	Supertax	Surtax	Total per cent	Normal tax.	Additional tax 1916	Additional tax 1917	Total
$5,000-$6,000	[1] 18.75-22.5	......	[1] 18.75-22.5	4	......	......	4	4	.....	1	5
$6,000-$7,500	[1] 18.75-22.5	......	[1] 18.75-22.5	4	2	.3	6.3	4	.....	1	5
$7,500-$10,000	[1] 22.5-26.25	......	[1] 22.5-26.25	4	2	.3	6.3	4	.....	2	6
$10,000-$12,500	[1] 26.25-30	5	[1] 31.25-35	4	5	9	9.9	4	.....	3	7
$12,500-$15,000	30	7.5	37.5	4	5	9	9.9	4	.....	4	8
$15,000-$20,000	30	10	40	4	5	9	9.9	4	.....	5	9
$20,000-$25,000	30	12.5	42.5	4	8	1.2	13.2	4	1	7	12
$25,000-$30,000	30	15	45	4	8	1.2	13.2	4	1	7	12
$30,000-$35,000	30	17.5	47.5	4	10	1.4	15.4	4	1	7	12
$35,000-$40,000	30	17.5	47.5	4	10	1.4	15.4	4	1	7	12
$40,000-$45,000	30	20	50	4	10	1.4	15.4	4	2	10	16
$45,000-$50,000	30	20	50	4	10	1.4	15.4	4	2	10	16
$50,000-$60,000	30	22.5	52.5	4	15	1.9	20.9	4	2	10	16
$60,000-$75,000	30	22.5	52.5	4	15	1.9	20.9	4	3	14	21
$75,000-$80,000	30	22.5	52.5	4	20	2.4	26.4	4	3	14	21
$80,000-$100,000	30	22.5	52.5	4	20	2.4	26.4	4	4	18	26
$100,000-$150,000	30	22.5	52.5	4	25	4.35	33.35	4	5	22	31
$150,000-$200,000	30	22.5	52.5	4	25	4.35	33.35	4	6	25	35
$200,000-$250,000	30	22.5	52.5	4	30	11.9	45.9	4	7	30	41
$250,000-$300,000	30	22.5	52.5	4	30	11.9	45.9	4	8	34	46
$300,000-$400,000	30	22.5	52.5	4	30	11.9	45.9	4	9	37	50
$400,000-$500,000	30	22.5	52.5	4	35	13.65	52.65	4	9	37	50
$500,000-$600,000	30	22.5	52.5	4	35	13.65	52.65	4	10	40	54
$600,000-$750,000	30	22.5	52.5	4	40	15.4	59.4	4	10	40	54
$750,000-$800,000	30	22.5	52.5	4	40	15.4	59.4	4	10	45	59
$800,000-$1,000,000	30	22.5	52.5	4	45	17.15	66.15	4	10	45	59
$1,000,000-$1,500,000	30	22.5	52.5	4	50	18.9	72.9	4	11	50	65
$1,500,000-$2,000,000	30	22.5	52.5	4	50	18.9	72.9	4	12	50	66
Over $2,000,000	30	22.5	52.5	4	50	18.9	72.9	4	13	50	67

[1] These rates apply only to the earned and unearned portions, respectively, of the whole income if its total amount is between the limits shown in column 1. In the case of incomes above $12,500 the full normal tax instead of these reduced rates is applied to the portions of income below $12,500.

FRANCE.

INCOME-TAX LAWS IN EFFECT JANUARY 1, 1918.

General Income Tax.

[Secs. 5–25 of the law of July 15, 1914, as amended by sec. 5 of the law of Dec. 30, 1916; the law of Feb. 23, 1917; and secs 49–50 of the law of July 31, 1917.]

(Journal Officiel, July 18, 1914, Dec. 31, 1916; Feb. 25, Aug. 1, 1917.)

Sec. 5. A general income tax is hereby imposed.

Sec. 6. The general income tax shall be due on the 1st of January of each year from all persons domiciled in France.

Any person shall be deemed to be domiciled in France who has a dwelling at his disposal there either as owner, occupier, or tenant: *Provided*, That in the last case the tenancy is one secured by a single lease or by successive leases for a continuous term of not less than one year.

Sec. 7. If a taxable person has only one residence, the tax shall be levied at the place of such residence.

If he has several residences, he shall be liable to the tax at the place known as his principal establishment.

Sec. 8. Every head of a family is liable both as regards his own income and that of his wife and other members of the family living with him: *Provided*, That taxable persons may request separate assessments:

(1) When a wife with a separate estate does not live with her husband.

(2) When the children or other members of the family, except the husband or wife, derive an income from their own work or from a fortune independent of that of the head of the family.

Sec. 9. The following are exempt from the tax:

(1) Persons whose taxable incomes do not exceed the sum of 3,000 francs, increased, if need be, as provided by section 12;

(2) Ambassadors and other foreign diplomatic agents, including consuls and consular agents of foreign nationality: *Provided*, That the countries they represent extend similar privileges to French diplomatic and consular agents.

Sec. 10. The tax shall be levied on the total amount of the net annual income of each taxable person. Such net income shall be determined with due regard to the personal and real property of the taxpayer, the professions exercised by him, the wages, salaries, pensions, and life annuities enjoyed by him, and the profits derived from any gainful occupation in which he may be engaged, after deducting:

(1) Interest on loans and debts owed by him.

(2) Arrears of the rents obligatorily due by him.

(3) All direct taxes or taxes assimilated thereto paid by him.

(4) Losses incurred in the conduct of any agricultural, commercial, or industrial enterprise.

The taxable income corresponding to the different sources of income enumerated above shall be determined every year on the basis of the receipts from each source during the preceding year.

In the case of incomes subject to a special tax levied by means of assessment lists, the taxable person shall have the right to determine the amount of such income according to the regulations fixed for the assessment of such special tax.

SEC. 11. Persons not living in France, although having one or more residences there, shall have their taxable income fixed at an amount equal to seven times the rental value of such residence or residences, unless the income derived by the taxable person from property, business, or profession, located or exercised in France, reaches a higher figure, in which case the latter shall constitute the basis for taxation.

SEC. 12. Married persons shall be entitled to an abatement of 2,000 francs from their annual income. In addition, every taxable person shall be entitled to an abatement of 1,000 francs for each person dependent on him, if the number of such persons does not exceed five. For each after the fifth, the abatement shall be 1,500 francs.

SEC. 13. The following shall be deemed to be persons dependent on the taxable person, provided they have no income distinct from that on which the latter is assessed:

(1) Parents and relatives over 70, or invalids.

(2) Descendants, or adopted children if under 21, or invalids.

SEC. 14. Each taxable person shall be taxed only on such part of his income as exceeds, after applying the provisions of section 12, the sum of 3,000 francs.

SEC. 15. The tax shall be computed by adding together—

One-tenth of the portion of the taxable income included between 3,000 and 8,000 francs;

Two-tenths of the portion included between 8,000 and 12,000 francs:

Three-tenths of the portion included between 12,000 and 16,000 francs;

Four-tenths of the portion included between 16,000 and 20,000 francs;

Five-tenths of the portion included between 20,000 and 40,000 francs;

Six-tenths of the portion included between 40,000 and 60,000 francs:

Seven-tenths of the portion included between 60,000 and 80,000 francs;

Eight-tenths of the portion included between 80,000 and 100,000 francs;

Nine-tenths of the portion included between 100,000 and 150,000 francs; and the whole of the excess of income beyond this;

and applying to the figure so obtained, the rate of 12.5 per cent.

On the tax so computed, every taxable person is entitled to a reduction of 5 per cent for one dependent, of 10 per cent for two dependents, of 20 per cent for three dependents, and so on, each dependent after the third entitling him to an additional reduction of 10 per cent: *Provided*, That the total reduction may not exceed one-half of the tax.

SEC. 16. Taxable persons shall make a return of their total income, giving full data as to the sources of such income.

They shall give in their return full information concerning those dependent on them.

In order to avail themselves of the deduction provided for by section 10, they must furthermore indicate in their return the amount and nature of the losses and debts which they have deducted from their total income, in accordance with section 10.

Returns shall be made on, or according to, forms prescribed by administrative regulation, and shall be filed within the first three months of each year.

Taxable persons failing to file a new return shall be deemed to to reaffirm their previous return.

Returns, duly signed, shall be left with, or mailed to, the collector of direct taxes, who shall acknowledge receipt of them.

SEC. 17. The collector shall verify the returns, and may request taxable persons to furnish explanations. He may correct returns: *Provided*, That in such case, before making any entry in the tax register, he shall notify the taxable person as to the data on which his assessment is to be based and grant him an opportunity to be heard, or to file his acceptance, or his objections, and to present such evidence as may be required whenever abatements are claimed under sections 10, 12, and 15. If disagreement still exists, legal relief may be sought by the taxable person, after publication of the assessment list.

If the insufficiency of an income return is detected after the setting up of the assessment list, the amount of tax corresponding to the deficiency may be claimed from the taxable person either in the same year or within the next five years.

If such claim is introduced, the court before which the case is brought shall examine the reasons presented by the authorities and by the taxable person and shall determine the basis for taxation, the burden of proof resting with the authorities.

SEC. 18. The amount of the tax shall be increased 10 per cent for any taxable person who fails to make a return within the period prescribed by section 16.

Wherever a taxable person has filed an understatement of his income, such person must pay, in addition to the taxes assessed against the real amount of his taxable income, a sum equal to the portion of the said taxes which corresponds to the income not declared: *Provided*, That such additional tax shall apply only in case the ascertained deficiency exceeds one-tenth of the taxable income.

SEC. 19. Any taxable person who fails to make a return or to reply to the request from the collector for explanations shall be taxed officially (*taxé d'office*[1]).

In case of disagreement with the tax administration, the person taxed officially may obtain discharge or abatement of the tax assessed against him in the courts only by presenting conclusive evidence proving the exact amount of his income, and bearing the cost of the proceedings, including examination fees. However, if his income, as determined by the proper authorities, should not exceed by more than 10 per cent the amount returned by him the costs shall be borne by the Government.

[1] The *taxation d'office* deprives the taxpayer of certain privileges and safeguards to which he is ordinarily entitled.

SEC. 20. If at the presentation of a will for probate a return or assessment is proved to be lacking or incomplete, the Treasury shall recover the unpaid taxes, increased in accordance with the provisions of section 18.

SEC. 21. The assessment list for the general income tax shall be prepared and the collection shall be made as in case of direct taxes.

In case of removal of the taxable person outside of the collection district, or in case of voluntary or compulsory sale, the tax shall be due immediately for the whole of the current year.

SEC. 22. Claims concerning the general income tax shall be filed, examined, and adjudicated in the same manner as those concerning direct taxes; *Provided*, That the said claims shall be adjudicated and the decisions rendered at a private hearing.

SEC. 23. All notices and communications relating to the income tax exchanged between agents of the administration or addressed by them to taxable persons must be sent in sealed envelopes.

Franking privileges and special rates of postage shall, when considered necessary, be granted or fixed by decree.

In accordance with the provisions of section 378 of the Penal Code, any person who, by reason of his functions or duties, is called upon to assist in assessing or collecting the tax or adjudicating claims, is bound to secrecy under penalties provided in the said section.

SEC. 24. Taxable persons shall not be entitled to procure any extracts from the general income-tax lists, in accordance with the laws and regulations governing direct taxes, except those referring to their own assessments.

SEC. 25. Such measures as may be necessary to carry into effect the provisions of sections 5 to 24 of this act shall be prescribed by administrative regulation.

TAXATION OF INDUSTRIAL AND COMMERCIAL PROFITS.

[Title I (secs. 2–15) of the law of July 31, 1917.]

SEC. 2. An annual tax is hereby imposed on the profits from commercial and industrial undertakings realized during the preceding year or during the period of 12 months as to which the last return was made, when such period does not coincide with the calendar year.

SEC. 3. The tax as to persons engaged in business shall be levied on the total amount of their undertakings in France at their place of management, or, in the absence thereof, at the principal place of business.

SEC. 4. The following are assessed on their net profits, after deducting all expenses, including the rental of the buildings used in the business and the amortization generally allowed according to the custom of each class of industry or trade:

Corporations or associations whose balance sheets must be presented to the registry office;

Taxable persons who have already declared the amount of their actual profits in connection with the assessment of the supertax on extraordinary profits realized during the war, as long as they are subject to such levy; also

All persons, corporations, or associations which, before the 1st of April of each year, have filed with the collector of direct taxes an abstract of their profit-and-loss account for the preceding year and have agreed, if occasion arises, to furnish in support thereof such proofs as may be required.

SEC. 5. For the purpose of assessing the taxable persons mentioned in the preceding section the collector may require them to furnish any data which he deems necessary. He shall hear the evidence of interested parties whose testimony he considers useful or who wish to make oral statements.

He shall determine the basis of the taxation, subject to appeal by the interested parties after publication of the assessment list.

SEC. 6. In the absence of the written statements referred to in section 4, the profits shall be computed by applying the proper coefficients to the volume of business.

A commission, appointed in the manner provided by section 8, shall determine the coefficients applicable to the different classes of taxable persons. The commission shall revise these coefficients every three years and shall decide what changes or additions have become necessary in the interval.

SEC. 7. For the purpose of determining the coefficients referred to in the preceding section, there may be established for each kind of business, several classes, according to the importance of the amount of business and of such other elements as are likely to influence productivity.

For each class thus established there shall be fixed either a single coefficient or a maximum and a minimum coefficient. In the latter case the collector shall have the right to determine, from the data at his disposal, the coefficient applicable to each taxable person within the limits of the corresponding maximum and minimum.

SEC. 8. The commission provided for by section 6 shall be established by decree rendered at the instance of the minister of finance.

One-fifth of its members shall be appointed on recommendation of presidents of boards of trade; another fifth shall be appointed on recommendation of the labor organizations of the different trades and industries. In the absence of such recommendations these two classes of members shall be appointed on recommendation of the minister of commerce and industry.

The commission shall be presided over by a councillor of state.

It may hear the evidence of any person having expert knowledge.

SEC. 9. The persons or corporations subject to the tax must, upon a demand made by the collector of direct taxes and sent by registered letter, make known in writing, within 20 days of the receipt of the said letter, the amount of their business in the course of the preceding year and furnish all necessary proof thereof.

If the taxable person refuses to comply with this demand, the collector shall proceed officially to appraise the amount of business, in which case the tax shall be increased by one-half.

SEC. 10. By means of the data gathered and of the inquiry conducted in accordance with the provisions of the preceding section, if such has been found necessary, the collector shall proceed to the provisional appraisal of the taxable income by applying to the amount of business the coefficient determined in the manner indicated in section 7: *Provided, however*, That when the collector is able to prove that the proportion of the actual net profits to the amount of business is greater than the single coefficient or than the minimum coefficient fixed by the commission, he may apply a higher coefficient, subject to the necessity of furnishing the proper proofs if his decision is called in question.

The collector shall communicate the results of the provisional appraisal to the interested parties, informing them that they are granted 20 days in which to present, in writing or verbally, any objections.

In case a taxable person is of the opinion that his taxable profits should be computed on the basis of a lower coefficient than the single coefficient or the minimum coefficient fixed by the commission, he may indicate what coefficient he thinks should be adopted and request its application, provided he furnish the necessary proofs.

As a result of the statements made, or upon the expiration of the term of 20 days above referred to, the collector shall decide finally upon the bases of the taxation, without prejudice to the right of the interested parties to lodge an appeal after the publication of the assessment list.

SEC. 11. In case of acknowledged incorrectness of the data furnished in conformity with sections 4, 9, and 10, the tax on that portion of the profits which has been concealed shall be doubled where the ascertained insufficiency is greater than one-tenth, or exceeds 20,000 francs.

If the insufficiency is detected after the assessment list is published, a supplementary assessment may be levied, either within the same year or in the course of the next five years.

SEC. 12. For the purpose of computing the tax that portion of the profits not exceeding 1,500 francs shall be reckoned as one quarter.

That portion between 1,500 and 5,000 francs as one-half.

The excess beyond this as the whole.

The rate of the tax is fixed at 4½ per cent.

SEC. 13. The following are subject to the tax on the profits derived from industrial and commercial undertakings, only on that portion of such profits which exceeds 1,500 francs:

Artisans working at home or for private persons without assistants or apprentices, whether as jobbers or on their own account and with material belonging to them, whether or not they have a sign or a shop;

Artisans working in a room with an apprentice less than 16 years of age;

A widow who continues with one workman or apprentice the trade of her deceased husband;

Itinerant vendors who sell wares of small value or common articles of food in streets, thoroughfares, or markets;

Fishermen, even though their boat belong to them.

The following are not considered as assistants or apprentices: Wives working with their husbands, unmarried children working with their parents, common laborers whose assistance is indispensable to the carrying on of the trade.

SEC. 14. Independently of the tax on the profits derived from industrial and commercial undertakings, as imposed by the preceding sections, a special tax [1] is imposed on the amount of business trans-

[1] This is to be distinguished from the retail sales tax imposed by secs. 23 to 26 of the act of Dec. 31, 1917, which is a tax of two-tenths of 1 per cent on retail sales of over 150 francs in value and is payable by the purchaser, the retailer merely acting as agent for the Government in collecting the tax, whereas the tax imposed by this section is payable by the retailer and is in effect an income tax, although the basis of assessment is the turnover rather than the net profits of his business.

acted by undertakings having for their principal object the retail sale of provisions or goods, when the amount of such business exceeds 1,000,000 francs, not including exports to foreign countries, to Algeria, or to [French] colonies and protectorates.

The tax is fixed in accordance with the following scale:

One-tenth per cent on that portion of the amount of business included between 1,000,000 and 2,000,000 francs.

Two-tenths per cent on that portion of the amount of business included between 2,000,001 and 10,000,000 francs.

Three-tenths per cent on that portion of the amount of business included between 10,000,001 and 100,000,000 francs.

Four-tenths per cent on that portion of the amount of business included between 100,000,001 and 200,000,000 francs.

Five-tenths per cent on that portion of the amount of business over 200,000,000 francs.

Taxable persons subject to the provisions of this section are required to file, within the first three months of each year, an annual return of the total amount of their business during the preceding year and to present such proofs as may be necessary to establish the accuracy of said return.

In case of failure to make the return, or of an incorrect return, the penalty provided by section 9, paragraph 2, of the present act shall be applied.

In the case of firms with numerous branches comprised under the class of undertakings referred to in the present section, the amount of business on which the special tax is to be assessed shall be the aggregate of the transactions of all the branches, whether located in the same city as the main establishment or in other cities.

SEC. 15. Cooperative associations owning establishments, stores, or shops for the sale or delivery of provisions, commodities, or goods, are subject to the tax on the profits derived from commercial and industrial undertakings, but not to the special tax imposed by section 14.

However, the following are exempted from the tax: Agricultural syndicates and cooperative associations which limit themselves to taking orders from their members and delivering from their warehouses the provisions, commodities, or goods so ordered; or which, selling to their members only, distribute annual bonuses to the said members or to public utilities, or lay aside said bonuses as a reserve fund not distributed among stockholders.

TAXATION OF AGRICULTURAL PROFITS.

[Title II (secs. 16–22) of the law of July 31, 1917.]

SEC. 16. An annual tax is hereby imposed on agricultural profits.

SEC. 17. The profits derived from agricultural undertakings are considered, for the purpose of assessing the tax, as equal to one-half the rental value of the land cultivated.

However, if the actual profits of the undertaking during the year preceding that of the taxation have been less than the figure adopted as the basis of taxation, the farm owners may, upon advancing the necessary proofs, obtain a proportional abatement of the tax by filing a claim after the publication of the assessment list.

SEC. 18. When the actual rental value of an agricultural undertaking does not exceed 12,000 francs, the farm owners shall pay the tax only on such portion of the income, computed in the manner set forth in the preceding section, as exceeds 1,250 francs.

He shall be entitled to an abatement:

Of two-thirds on the portion of the income between 1,251 and 2,000 francs;

And of one-third on the portion of the income between 2,001 and 3,000 francs.

The rate of the tax is fixed at 3.75 per cent.

SEC. 19. The tax shall be levied on farm owners at their principal domicile on January 1 of the taxable year on the basis of the extent of their undertakings on that date.

SEC. 20. The assessment list for the tax on agricultural profits shall be prepared and the collection carried out as in the case of direct taxes.

Removal of a taxable person beyond the jurisdiction of the collecting office, or voluntary or compulsory sale, shall cause the tax to fall due at once for the whole of the current year.

SEC. 21. Claims concerning the tax on agricultural profits shall be filed, examined, and adjudicated as in the case of direct taxes: *Provided, however,* That claims presented in accordance with paragraph 2 of section 17 shall be adjudicated and the decisions pronounced at private hearings; furthermore, notices and communications relative thereto shall be transmitted in the manner provided by section 23 of the act of July 15, 1914, concerning the general income tax.

SEC. 22. Parks, gardens, avenues, ornamental waters, and all lands reserved for pleasure only or especially kept for hunting are subject to the tax on agricultural profits on the basis of an income to be determined in the manner provided by paragraph 1 of section 17.

The tax shall be computed on the whole of such income, without abatement or allowance of any kind.

Persons enjoying the possession of private parks, gardens, or game preserves whose area does not exceed one hectare and whose taxable income is not over 100 francs shall be exempt from the tax.

TAXATION OF SALARIES, WAGES, PENSIONS, ANNUITIES, ETC.

[Title III (secs. 23–29) of the law of July 31, 1917.]

SEC. 23. Pensions, life annuities, and the income derived from public and private salaries, allowances, fees, and wages shall be subject to a tax levied on that portion of their yearly total which exceeds the following amounts:

1. In the case of pensions and life annuities, 1,250 francs.
2. In the case of salaries, allowances, fees, and wages—

1,500 francs, if the taxable person lives in a commune of less than 10,001 inhabitants;

2,000 francs, if the taxable person lives in a commune of 10,001 to 100,000 inhabitants;

2,500 francs, if the taxable person lives in a commune of more than 100,000 inhabitants;

3,000 francs, if the taxable person lives in Paris, in the department of the Seine, or in suburban towns within a radius of 25 kilometers of the Paris fortifications: *Provided, however,* That in computing the tax, only one-half of the portion of the taxable income included between the exempted minimum and the sum of 5,000 francs shall be considered.

The rate of the tax is fixed at 3.75 per cent.

SEC. 24. In determining the basis of the taxation, the actual net amount of the salaries, allowances or fees, wages, pensions, or life annuities shall be taken into account, as well as all gratuities in money or in kind granted to the interested parties over and above their salaries, allowances or fees, wages, pensions, or life annuities proper.

SEC. 25. The tax shall be due each year on salaries, allowances or fees, wages, pensions or life annuities received during the preceding year.

It shall be levied upon the said forms of income at the commune where the taxable persons have their domicile on January 1 of the taxable year.

SEC. 26. All persons, associations, or corporations having employees, clerks, workmen, or laborers who receive a salary, wages, or pay, must file, with the collector of direct taxes, some time in January of each year, a return showing:

1. The names and addresses of the persons they have had in their employ during the preceding year;

2. The amount of the salaries, wages, and pay received by each one of such persons during the said year;

3. The period as to which such payments were made when for less than a year, and for more than 30 consecutive days.

The preceding provisions, however, shall apply only to persons whose salary, wages, or pay, computed on a yearly basis in accordance with the provisions of the present act, exceeds the minimum subject to the tax.

SEC. 27. All persons, associations, or corporations paying pensions or life annuities must furnish information similar to that provided for in the preceding section relative to the holders of such pensions or life annuities as exceed 1,250 francs.

SEC. 28. Using the data furnished in accordance with the preceding provisions, as well as any other which he may be able to collect, the collector of direct taxes shall fix the basis of assessment, without prejudice, however, to the right of the parties concerned to contest his decision after the publication of the assessment list.

SEC. 29. Each omission or misstatement in the data furnished in accordance with sections 26 and 27 shall make the offender liable to a fine of 5 francs.

The fine shall be imposed by the council of the prefecture, acting as in the matter of breach of regulations, upon request presented without cost by the director of direct taxes.

A copy of the request shall be delivered to the offenders through the council of the prefecture.

Proceedings may not be instituted after the expiration of the fourth year following that in which the violation took place.

The fine shall be collected by the collector of direct taxes.

TAXATION OF PROFESSIONAL INCOMES.

[Title IV (secs. 30–37) of the law of July 31, 1917.]

SEC. 30. The incomes from liberal professions and other non-mercantile offices and employments, as well as from all lucrative occupations and undertakings not liable to a special income tax, shall be subject to a tax levied annually upon the net income for the preceding year, consisting of the excess of total receipts over expenses incurred.

SEC. 31. The tax shall be levied only on that portion of the net profits in excess of the sum of:

One thousand five hundred francs, if the taxable person lives in a commune of less than 10,001 inhabitants;

Two thousand francs, if the taxable person lives in a commune of from 10,001 to 100,000 inhabitants;

Two thousand five hundred francs, if the taxable person lives in a commune of over 100,000 inhabitants;

Three thousand francs, if the taxable person lives in Paris, in the Department of the Seine, or in suburban towns within a radius of 25 kilometers of the Paris fortifications: *Provided, however,* That for the purpose of computing the tax, that portion of the net profits included between the exempted minimum and the sum of 5,000 francs shall be divided in half.

The rate of tax is fixed at 3.75 per cent.

Nothing, however, contained in the preceding provisions shall be held to prevent the tax upon such of the offices and employments mentioned in section 30 as are mercantile in character from being computed in the manner and according to the rate fixed by section 12.

SEC. 32. The tax shall be due in the commune where the taxable person resides on January 1 of the taxable year.

SEC. 33. All persons liable to the tax on incomes derived from any of the occupations referred to in section 30 must, within the first three months of each year, make a return of the amount of their incomes.

SEC. 34. The return shall be addressed to the collector of direct taxes of the place of residence of the taxable person, and a receipt delivered therefor.

SEC. 35. The collector shall take as the basis of the assessment the amount of income as declared, unless he knows that it is incorrect. In the latter case he may correct it. But he must, before fixing the amount of the tax, make known to the person concerned the figure which he intends to substitute for that given in the return. He must state his grounds for making the correction, and must at the same time request the person concerned to submit his objections, if he so desires, within 20 days, in writing or verbally. If the disagreement persists, the taxable person shall retain the right to contest, after the publication of the assessment list, the figure decided upon by the collector. The court to which the controversy is referred shall weigh the considerations set forth by the administration and by the taxable person, taking into account, if necessary, the obligations of professional secrecy, and shall fix the basis of the taxation.

SEC. 36. Any taxable person under obligation to make the return referred to in section 30 who fails to do so within the first three months of the year shall be asked by the collector to file such return within 20 days. After the lapse of such period the taxable income shall, subject to appeal by the taxable person after the publication of the assessment list, be officially assessed. But in that case the tax shall be increased by one-half.

SEC. 37. If a return is proved to be incorrect, the tax on that portion of the income which has been concealed shall be doubled. This shall, however, only take place where the proved discrepancy involves over one-tenth of the actual income or exceeds 10,000 francs.

If the discrepancy is discovered after publication of the assessment list, a supplementary payment may be demanded of the taxable person, either in the same year or within the next five years.

Taxation of Incomes from Transferable Securities.

[Title II (secs. 31–39, 42, 47) of the law of Mar. 29, 1914, as amended by the law of Dec. 30, 1916, sec. 11.]

Sec. 31. The tax on incomes derived from securities shall apply to dividends, interest, payments of annuities, and all other income derived—

1. From stocks, deferred stocks, interests (not divided into shares), limited partnerships ("*commandites*"), debentures, and loans of whatever description of French companies or corporations referred to in section 1 of the act of June 29, 1872, and not exempted by subsequent laws from the tax on incomes derived from transferrable securities:

2. From stocks, deferred stocks, interests (not divided into shares), limited partnerships ("*commandites*"), debentures, and loans of whatever description of foreign companies, associations, undertakings, corporations, cities, provinces, as well as of all other foreign public institutions:

3. From bonds, annuities, or other public securities of the French colonies and of foreign governments.

Sections 3 and 4 of the act of December 28, 1880; section 9 of the act of December 29, 1884; section 4 of the act of December 26, 1890; sections 3 to 10 of the act of April 16, 1895; section 20 of the act of February 25, 1901; section 12 of the act of July 13, 1911, shall remain in force.

Sec. 32. The interest, dividends, payments of annuities, or any other income accruing from the securities specified by section 31 are for the purposes of levying the income tax to be ascertained in accordance with the provisions of section 2 of the act of June 29, 1872.

Sec. 33. The tax on incomes derived—

1. From the French securities referred to in paragraph 1 of section 31;

2. From those of the foreign securities referred to in paragraph 2 of the same section which are subject, under existing laws, to duties or taxes equivalent to those levied on French securities;

3. From bonds, annuities, or other public securities of the French colonies—

shall be assessed and levied on the basis fixed and subject to the conditions prescribed by the acts of June 29, 1872, and of June 21, 1875, and by subsequent enactments. The rate of the tax is fixed at 5 per cent.

Sec. 34. In the case of those of the foreign securities included under paragraph 2 of section 31 which are not subject, under existing laws, to duties or taxes equivalent to those levied on French securities, and in the case of bonds, loans, and other public securities of foreign governments, the obligation to collect the tax is laid on the banker, money changer, or any other person who in France effects payments of interest, annuity charges, or other increments.

SEC. 35. Anyone whose profession or business it is to collect, receive, buy, or sell coupons, checks, or any other instrument of credit established for the payment of dividends, interest, annuities, or increment of whatever description derived from bonds or securities described in the preceding section, must declare the same at the registration office of his place of residence.

When, owing to existing contracts, the tax is payable by the party issuing the security, all persons referred to in paragraph 1 of this section are prohibited from collecting, receiving, buying, or selling the coupons, checks, or other instruments of credit referred to in the said paragraph, unless the tax is immediately collected or advance payment thereof is made, or unless they receive evidence that such collection or advance payment was already made by a prior agent subject to the provisions of this and of the following sections.

SEC. 36. Any one laying claim to payment of his coupons, checks, or instruments of credit in France shall file at the same time in support of his claim a dated memorandum, for which receipt may be demanded. This memorandum shall bear neither the name, signature, nor address of the person filing it.

The person making the payment shall enter at once upon the memorandum the amount of the tax collected or paid in advance.

The persons mentioned in section 35 who negotiate coupons, checks, or other instruments of credit on which the tax has already been collected either by themselves or by a prior agent, must in support of each transfer append a dated and signed memorandum.

The said persons must keep two registers of unstamped paper, numbered and initialed, on which they must enter every day, without blank spaces or interlineation, all transactions involving payment, purchase, or sale of the coupons, checks, or other instruments of credit subject to tax.

The registers and memoranda shall be kept on file for two years and shall be open to inspection by registration officers.

An administrative order shall provide for the times for payment of the tax, the information which the memoranda must contain, the acknowledgments of receipt and the registers, the amount of abatements and their mode of payment, as well as all other measures required to enforce the provisions contained in this section and in sections 34 and 35.

SEC. 37. Any holder or recipient of income from foreign shares or securities who is domiciled in France and who shall have sent to him or shall receive abroad, whether directly or through an intermediary, the dividends, interest, payments of annuity, or any other increment accruing from such bonds or securities shall be required, when receiving the first annual coupons, to affix upon each share a special adhesive stamp for an amount equivalent to the 4 per cent tax on the entire year's income. If he fails to conform to the preceding provisions, the aforesaid holder or recipient of income shall, within the first three months of the year, make a declaration at the registration office of the total amount of such dividends, interest, payments of annuity, or increment received in the course of the preceding year, and to pay the tax on the aggregate amount.

All persons violating the provisions contained in the preceding paragraph shall be punished by a fine equal to five times the amount lost to the Treasury during each year previous to the discovery of the violation: *Provided, however*, That the right to recover such amount may not extend over a period of more than 10 years.

SEC. 38. Officials of the registration office and of courts of law, police and customs officers, and those concerned with the administration of direct and of indirect taxes, shall report in writing violations of the provisions contained in section 35 and of the regulations to be issued in execution of the said section.

Proceedings shall be instituted on request of the registration department against offenders, who shall be liable to a fine of from 100 to 1,000 francs, in addition to the payment of five times the duty on coupons, checks, or instruments of credit that were paid without collection of the tax.

The proceeds of the fines mentioned in this section shall be distributed in such manner as shall be determined by decree.

Violations of section 36 or 37 or of the regulations to be issued in execution of said sections shall be recorded and proceeded against as in the case of taxes on stock-exchange transactions and shall be punished by a fine of from 100 to 10,000 francs.

Violations of the provisions contained in paragraph 1 of section 35 shall, if the offender, whether acting in his own name or in behalf of another, has no domicile in France, entail criminal proceedings and render such offender liable to imprisonment for six months to one year and to a fine of 1,000 to 10,000 francs, and, upon repetition of the offense, to imprisonment for one to two years and to a fine of 10,000 to 25,000 francs.

SEC. 39. Proceedings shall be instituted for the recovery of the tax upon the income from transferable securities, and action brought and adjudicated as in the matter of registration, subject to such procedure as shall be adopted in respect of the violations referred to in paragraph 1 of the preceding section.

The provisions of section 21 of the act of July 26, 1893, shall be applicable, respectively, to suits brought by the Treasury and by taxable persons, with the exception of the case contemplated in section 37.

* * * * * * *

SEC. 42. The foreign securities enumerated in section 5, paragraphs 1 and 2 of the act of December 28, 1895, * * * are, in addition to the tax provided for in section 31 liable to a supplementary annual income tax of 1 per cent to be collected on the same basis and subject to the same conditions.

* * * * * * *

SEC. 47. Measures in execution of the sections included in part 2 of this act shall be provided for by administrative order.

[Title V (secs. 38–43) of the law of July 31, 1917.]

SEC. 38. The tax on the income derived from securities established by sections 31 and following of the act of March 29, 1914, the rate of which was modified by section 11 of the act of December 30, 1916, shall apply to the interest, arrears, and all other revenues accruing from:

1. Mortgages in writing, excluding any commercial transactions not recognized by law as loans;

2. Deposits of money repayable on demand within a given time, whoever the depositor may be and whatever the purpose of the deposit;

3. Money deposited as security.

SEC. 39. There shall be exempted from the tax on income derived from securities:

1. The interest on the sums entered in savings banks' pass books;

2. The interest on mortgage indebtedness to cover which associations or companies authorized by the Government to engage in real estate loan operations have issued bonds, shares, or securities, which are subject to the income tax.

SEC. 40. The tax shall be paid out of the gross amount of the interest, arrears, or other revenues referred to in section 38 above.

The payment of the tax on the said securities shall be indicated by affixing a stamp to the receipt or other writing which certifies that the interest, arrears, or other increment has been paid to the taxable person or credited to his account.

The tax shall in every case be payable by the creditor, notwithstanding any agreement to the contrary of whatsoever date; the creditor and the debtor are, however, jointly and severally liable.

Any violation of the provisions of the present section shall be punished by a fine of 50 francs payable by each offender, exclusive of the payment by the creditor of a fine equal to five times the amount withheld from the Treasury during each year prior to that in which the discovery of the infringement was made: *Provided, however,* That the right of recovery may not extend over more than ten years.

SEC. 41. The collection of the tax on the income derived from securities shall be made, and claims shall be filed and adjudicated as in the case of registration.

The provisions of section 21 of the act of July 26, 1893, shall be respectively applicable to the actions brought by the Treasury or by the debtors, with the exception of the case mentioned in the last paragraph of section 40.

SEC. 42. The owner of real estate encumbered by mortgage, pledge, or assignment of revenue, as guarantee for a debt, shall obtain on demand abatement of part of the land tax. The abatement shall consist of that part of the Government's share of the tax which is levied on income from such real estate equal in amount to the interest on the debt guaranteed.

The demand for abatement shall be filed, examined, and adjudicated as in the case of direct taxes. It must be made within three months of the date of payment of the interest and accompanied by the receipt or release duly stamped as provided in section 40.

The interest on debts arising from a written contract shall be deducted from the income of the debtor, excepting those as to which securities have been issued.

In order to avail themselves of this abatement, the persons subject to the tax must ask for it and prove that the debt really exists; that the interest on the alleged debt has in fact been paid to the creditor, and has been subjected to the tax referred to in section 38.

The abatement shall apply first to the income from the undertaking or working on account of which the debt has been contracted. If said income is insufficient, or if proof of the origin of the debt is lacking, the abatement shall apply to other classes of income, beginning with the least heavily taxed.

Whenever securities have been assigned as a pledge to secure a debt, the debtor may obtain repayment of a portion of the income tax on the said securities, equal in amount to the tax collected on the interest of his debt: *Provided*, That (1) he present the request and proofs referred to in paragraph 4 of the present section, and (2) that he prove that the tax on the income from the pledged securities devolves upon the holder of such securities and has been paid by him.

SEC. 43. An administrative order shall prescribe such measures as may be necessary to carry into effect the sections included under Title V of this act.

TAXATION OF INCOME FROM IMPROVED AND UNIMPROVED REAL ESTATE.

[Title I (secs. 1–30) of the law of Mar. 29, 1914, as amended by the law of July 31, 1917, secs. 47–48.]

(Journal Officiel, Mar. 31 1914; Aug. 1, 1917.)

TAX ON UNIMPROVED REAL ESTATE.

BASES OF THE TAX.

SECTION 1. After January 1, 1915, the land tax on unimproved real estate shall cease to be an apportioned tax, and the quotas to be paid by the departments, arrondissements, and communes shall no longer be fixed.

SEC. 2. After that date the land tax on unimproved real estate shall be assessed in proportion to the income derived therefrom as determined by existing rates, according to the nature of the crops or of the property itself, in pursuance of section 3 of the act of December 31, 1907, and of the rules laid down in the ministerial circular of December 31, 1908. For the purpose of computing the tax, the income shall be estimated at one-fifth less than its actual amount.

SEC. 3. The ground under buildings of whatever description and the land appurtenant thereto shall no longer be liable to the land tax on unimproved real estate; the rental value of such ground or land shall, however, be taken into account in computing the income on which such portion of the land tax on improved real estate as relates to buildings is based.

SEC. 4. The provisions of the preceding section relating to the ground under buildings shall be applicable to parcels of land used for commercial or industrial purposes. Such land shall continue to be liable to the land tax on improved real estate imposed by section 1 of the act of December 29, 1884.

SEC. 5. When a piece of property becomes liable to the land tax on unimproved real estate, whether for the first time or after having temporarily ceased to be so liable, especially where such property ceases to belong to the class of land referred to in sections 3 and 4 of this act, the value of said property shall be assessed on the basis of rates applicable to similar property existing in the commune, or, in the absence of such property, on the basis of rates adopted by comparison with rates applicable to other properties.

RATE OF THE TAX.

SEC. 6. The rate of the tax on unimproved real estate is hereby fixed at 5 per cent of the taxable income of such properties, to be determined as stated in section 2 of this act.

REVISION OF THE ASSESSMENT

SEC. 7. The assessments on which the land tax on unimproved real estate is based shall be revised in each commune every 20 years.

For this purpose the communes of each department shall be divided into 20 groups and every year assessments shall be revised in the communes of one of these groups.

The distribution of the communes among the 20 groups shall be regulated by the prefect, upon recommendation of the [departmental] director of direct taxes and land survey; in case of disagreement between the prefect and the director, the Minister of Finance shall decide.

The order in which the revision of the 20 groups is to take place shall be determined by the General Council[1] at its first session of the year 1918. If the General Council does not meet, or if it adjourns without deciding the matter, the order shall be determined by the prefect in the manner described in the preceding paragraph.

Whenever a new commune is created the prefect shall select the group to which it is to be assigned for future revisions.

SEC. 8. At the time of the revision of assessments in each commune the rates of assessment and the classification of the parcels according to the nature of crops and of the property itself shall be fixed by the comptroller of direct taxes, assisted by the mayor and by five assessors. The assessors must be landowners; at least two of them must be nonresident; and they must be appointed by the prefect from a list of 10 names submitted by the municipal council. When wooded property included within a commune covers an area of not less than 100 hectares,[2] the commission must include at least one assessor who is an owner of wood or forest land. In assessing wooded property the said assessor shall, upon demand of the Department of Waters and Forests, be assisted by an official of the forestry service.

In the absence of a selective list, the assessors shall be officially appointed by the prefect, one month after the meeting of the municipal council has been called.

In Paris, the members of the commission on direct taxes shall act as assessors.

One or more extra employees, appointed by the prefect and paid by the commune, may be named to assist in the work of revising assessments, either on demand of the municipal council, or by administrative order when the assessors refuse to undertake such revision.

SEC. 9. Whenever the local administration of direct taxes, in cooperation with the assessors, is unable to determine rates of assessments according to the nature of crops and of the property itself, such rates shall be fixed by a commission established in every department, to consist of—

The prefect, chairman;

---

[1] The General Council is the legislative assembly of a department and corresponds, with certain limitations, to a State legislature It holds two sessions yearly.

[2] 1 hectare=2.4711 acres.

Two members of the General Council to be designated each year for the following year by the General Council, in the course of its second session, or, if it fails to act, by the prefect;

The treasurer general;[1]

The director of direct taxes and land survey;

The director of registration, public property, and stamps;

The departmental director of agriculture;

A representative of an agricultural society, or a farmer, appointed every year by the prefect;

The inspector of direct taxes and land survey, acting as secretary.

The rates, as determined by the service of direct taxes in cooperation with the assessors, or by the commission established by this section, shall, through the director of direct taxes and land survey, be communicated to the mayor, and the latter shall, within five days from such notification, cause said rates to be posted at the door of the town hall, and shall send to the said director official notice that this formality has been complied with.

SEC. 10. Within a month following the posting of the rates, the mayor, if duly authorized by the municipal council, and the director of direct taxes and land survey, are each entitled to appeal from the decisions of the commission referred to in the preceding section to a central commission, whose decision shall be final. Such commission, established in the ministry of finance, shall consist of—

The minister of finance, or his representative, chairman;

One senator and two deputies, appointed by decree;

The director general of public accounting, or his representative;

The director general of direct taxes and land survey, or his representative;

The director general of registration, public property, and stamps, or his representative;

An official of the ministry of agriculture, named by the minister of agriculture.

A high official of the general administration of direct taxes and land survey, named by the minister of finance, shall act as secretary, with the right to advise but not to vote.

One or more employees of the general administration of direct taxes and land survey may, moreover, be named by the minister of finance to attend the meetings of the commission as assistant secretaries.

SEC. 11. The landowners concerned are also entitled, on the same conditions and within the same time prescribed in the preceding section, to contest the rate applicable to a given class of crops or of property. But the petition filed in support of such objection shall only be admissible if the signatory or signatories of the protest are the owners of more than one-half of the area of the land to which the rate objected to is applicable.

SEC. 12. Upon the completion of assessments, property owners shall be notified. Within a month of the receipt of the notice thus mailed to them, they may make application for a duplicate detailed account of such of the assessing operations as relate to their properties. The said property owners shall be granted a period of two months

[1] The treasurer general is an official performing, in the capital of a department, the functions of special collector of finances for the department.

from the date of the receipt of such duplicate account, or of three months from the receipt of the first notice, within which to file their objections. These objections shall be referred to the board of assessment.

The notice informing the landowner of the assessed valuation of his properties shall include the text of this section.

SEC. 13. In every commune the mayor, duly authorized by the municipal council, may apply to the prefect any time before June 30, 1917, for the reassessment of unimproved real estate. Such application shall be successively referred to the two commissions established by sections 9 and 10. If it is approved by them, the minister of finance shall have power to direct such reassessment to be made, and the same rules as apply to the vicennial revisions shall apply to said reassessment.

Property owners also may before that date demand the revision of rates applicable to a given class of crops or property: *Provided, however*, That the signatory or signatories of the petition must own over one-half of the area of the land to which the disputed rates apply. The procedure in the case of such petition shall be the same as that prescribed in the preceding paragraph.

After July 1, 1917, a request for the revision of the assessments in any commune may be made only by the mayor, when authorized by the municipal council, and only in case exceptional circumstances have arisen since the last assessment causing all real estate or an important percentage thereof to undergo a serious general depreciation. The request for such revision shall be subject to the procedure set forth in paragraph 1 of this section, and the costs of the reassessment shall be borne by the commune.

If in the communes in which the provisions of the preceding paragraph are applied, a substantial increase in the value of the real estate later takes place, the minister of finance may direct that a fresh revision of the assessments be made before the termination of the current vicennial period.

The assessments fixed in accordance with this section shall only serve as a basis for the tax in the rolls of the years following that of the completion of the work. Such assessments shall in any case be revised at the end of the current vicennial period, in accordance with section 7, as if there had been no special revision.

SEC. 14. When surveying operations are undertaken, revised, or renewed in a commune, completion of the measurements shall be followed by a general valuation of the unimproved real estate as provided for by sections 8 to 12 above. The results of such valuation shall constitute the basis of the land tax for the rolls of the years following the completion of the survey until the results of the nearest periodical revision are applied.

CLAIMS.

SEC. 15. Every landowner may, within six months after the publication of the assessment list established on the basis of the results of the first valuation, or within three months after the publication of the next assessment list, contest the classification of the nature of crops or of the property itself to which his real estate is made subject.

SEC. 16. A claim made in pursuance of the foregoing provisions, even if made with respect to no more than one of the parcels appraised in a section of the assessment list, may cause the nature of the crops or the classification erroneously assigned to other parcels included in the same section to be corrected: *Provided, however,* That the assessment entered in the said section may not be increased thereby. To this end recommendations accompanied by a report of the assessing commission referred to in section 8, shall, if the case require, be made by the administration to the court before which the case is laid, and said court shall pass upon such recommendations at the same time as upon the claimant's request.

SEC. 17. The right of property owners to file objections following each revision that may take place in accordance with sections 7, 13, and 14 of this act shall be exercised under the same conditions and within the same periods of time as those fixed by sections 15 and 16. The same procedure shall be observed in the case of property assessed in the manner provided for by section 5; but in the latter case the provisions of section 16 shall not be applicable.

SEC. 18. Property owners shall be authorized to request a change in the classification of their property when such property has undergone a serious and permanent depreciation as a result of unexpected events beyond the control of the persons concerned and affecting the very soil of the land. Claims brought on such a basis shall be admissible within six months after the publication of the assessment list for the year following that in which the events they refer to have taken place.

SEC. 19. With the exception of the cases mentioned in sections 15 to 18 and those which, under existing laws, may justify a temporary tax exemption, no application for remission or abatement of the tax on unimproved real estate shall be admissible, except where property ceases to be of a taxable nature or comes under the same category as the property referred to in sections 3 and 4 of this act.

SEC. 20. Objections relating to the tax on unimproved real estate shall be filed, examined, and passed upon as in the case of the tax on improved real estate.

TAX ON IMPROVED REAL ESTATE.

RATE OF THE TAX.

SEC. 21. After January 1, 1915, the rate of the land tax on improved real estate shall be fixed at 4 per cent of the net income derived therefrom as determined in accordance with existing provisions.

REVISION OF THE ASSESSMENTS.

SEC. 22. In every department, the [twenty] groups of communes formed for the periodical revaluation of the income derived from unimproved real estate shall be arranged in pairs, and every year, the decennial revaluation prescribed by section 8 of the act of August 8, 1890, for the income derived from improved real estate shall be applied to one of these ten series of groups. These series of groups shall be so constituted and arranged that in every commune the revaluation of the income derived from improved real estate shall take place every ten years, and that in any commune in which the revaluation of the income derived from unimproved real estate is to take place, the revaluation of the income derived from improved real estate shall be effected the same year.

At the time of the periodical revision provided for in the foregoing paragraph, the fixtures of industrial establishments permanently attached to the land in the manner set forth in paragraph 1 of article 525 of the Civil Code, or resting upon special foundations attached to the building, shall be regarded as liable to the tax on improved real estate. The provisions of section 12 of this act shall be applicable to improved real estate. As regards industrial establishments, the detailed account shall comprise two separate sets of figures, one concerning the building, the other that portion of the fixtures liable to the tax on improved real estate.

SEC. 23. However, in cities whose aggregate civil population, as determined by the census decree in force at the time of the promulgation of this act, exceeds 50,000 inhabitants, the valuations assigned to improved real estate shall be revised at the expiration of the decennial period beginning at the time of the last revision effected in pursuance of the act of August 8, 1890, and thereafter at the expiration of each successive period of 10 years.

SEC. 24. In the event of the establishment, revision, or renewal of the land survey in the commune a fresh valuation of the income derived from improved real estate shall be made in accordance with existing laws, and the results of such valuation shall serve as the basis for the land tax in the manner set forth in section 14 with respect to unimproved real estate.

CENTIMES ADDITIONAL TO THE LAND TAX.[1]

CENTIMES ACCRUING TO THE GOVERNMENT.

SEC. 25. Beginning with 1915 centimes additional to the principal amount of the tax on improved and unimproved real estate shall no longer be collected in behalf of the Government.

The Government's quota of the said tax shall only consist, in addition to the principal tax, of centimes on account of unpaid taxes computed on the basis of the departmental and communal quotas and of centimes to defray the cost of collecting communal taxes.

DEPARTMENTAL AND COMMUNAL CENTIMES.

SEC. 26. The principal amount serving each year, beginning with 1915, as the basis on which the total amount per commune of the departmental centimes additional to the taxes on improved and unimproved real estate is to be calculated shall consist for all communes of each department of a fixed proportion of the total taxable revenue. This proportion shall be the average proportion for all the communes of each department, and for the two taxes together, between the amount which, according to the provisions in force prior to the passage of this act, would have served as basis in 1915 for the calculation of the local taxes, and the corresponding amount of taxable revenue actually included in the general lists for the said year.

[1] The centime is a surtax collectible at the same time and by the same means as the principal tax

The total amount of these centimes additional to the land tax shall in each commune be calculated according to the same principal amounts followed in calculating the total amounts of departmental centimes in application of the foregoing paragraph.

SEC. 27. The General Council shall, however, have the right to decide, in the course of its second session of 1914, that, notwithstanding the provisions of the foregoing section, the equal distribution provided for in said section of the principal amounts serving as a basis for the calculation of the local taxes shall, beginning with 1915, instead of being arrived at at one time, be effected by successive stages: *Provided, however,* That the length of the transitional period shall not exceed 10 years.

MISCELLANEOUS PROVISIONS.

SEC. 28. In communes where, after the valuation made in pursuance of the act of December 31, 1907, and before this act takes effect, a general valuation of unimproved real estate has been made in accordance with the laws and regulations concerning land surveying, the results of such valuation (which shall previously be modified in such manner as to take into account the rules laid down in sections 2 to 4 above referred to) shall be taken as the basis of the land tax for 1915 and after, in lieu of the results of the valuation made in pursuance of the act of December 31, 1907.

SEC. 29. The year 1920 is hereby fixed as the time when the periodical revisions provided for by sections 7 and 22, above referred to, shall first be applied both to improved and unimproved real estate.

Until such revisions have taken place in all the communes, the period during which the valuations shall hold good, fixed by section 8 of the act of August 8, 1890, and by section 7 of this act, may be either shortened or extended, as may be required to insure a regular sequence of the work of revision.

SEC. 30. Legislative enactments concerning the land tax, not contrary to this act, shall remain in force.

Whenever the taxable income of the whole of the unimproved property owned by a landowner engaged in farming on his own account does not exceed 400 francs and his total income does not exceed 1,250 francs, such landowner shall be entitled to the discharge of so much of the land tax levied on the real property which he both owns and cultivates as equals in amount the tax collectible on a taxable income of 200 francs.

In order to obtain the discharge mentioned in the preceding paragraph, the taxable person must file at the town hall of his actual domicile a return in writing indicating, according to the land survey, all the unimproved lands owned by him and such as he cultivates in person, declaring at the same time that his total income does not exceed 1,250 francs; such declaration shall be assumed to be correct, unless evidence to the contrary is brought forward by the administration.

The declarations must be filed every year, before the 10th of February. Taxable persons are not required to revise them yearly, but such facts as may necessitate correction of the data contained in said declarations must form the subject of additional declarations before the 10th of February of the following year.

68422—18——4

Such declarations as the comptroller of direct taxes, together with the mayor and the assessors, may approve, shall be entered in a special register, after examining which the director of direct taxes shall each year grant such abatements as are in his opinion justifiable.

Taxable persons whose declarations have been rejected shall be informed of the fact, and they shall have the right to make application for abatement in the usual manner within a month after receipt of the notice mailed to them.

If the declaration contains false statements likely to result in the taxable person being granted an abatement exceeding that which he may legally claim, such person shall forego his right to an abatement for the current year.

Whoever shall knowingly, whether by means of an incorrect declaration or through omitting to correct a previous declaration, fraudulently obtain, or try to obtain, the abatements mentioned in this section, shall be liable to a fine of 50 to 100 francs, which may be doubled in case of repetition of the offense.

The fine shall be imposed by the council of the prefecture, deciding as in the case of contraventions, on petition made without cost by the director of direct taxes and land survey. Such petition, which shall be accompanied by a certified duplicate copy of the declaration, shall serve as the official record required by the acts of May 30, 1851, and July 22, 1889.

A duplicate copy of the petition shall be mailed to the offender by the council of the prefecture.

The right to prosecute shall expire by limitation at the end of the fourth year following that in which an abatement has been fraudulently obtained or asked for.

The fine shall be recovered by the collector as in the case of direct taxes.

Miscellaneous Provisions.

[Applicable to the Scheduled Income Taxes.]

[Secs. 51–55 of the law of July 31, 1917.]

Sec. 51. The provisions of sections 21 to 24 of the act of July 15, 1914, concerning the general income tax shall apply to the taxes created by the present act on profits from commercial and industrial undertakings; on public and private salaries, allowances and fees, wages, pensions and life annuities; and on the profits derived from pursuits other than commercial.

Sec. 52. Every taxable person shall be entitled to an abatement on the Government's share of the land tax and on such of the income taxes established by the present act as are levied by means of assessment lists. The amount of the abatement shall be: 5 per cent for one dependent, 10 per cent for two dependents, 20 per cent for three dependents, and for each dependent after the third an increased abatement of 10 per cent: *Provided, however,* That the total abatement may not exceed one-half of the amount of the tax.

Persons described in section 13 of the general income-tax act of July 15, 1914, shall be considered as dependents.

In order to avail themselves of the foregoing provisions, taxable persons must send to the collector of their residence a declaration giving the name and forename, date, and place of birth of every person dependent on them, together with such information as to kinship, etc., as may show that said persons come within the purview of the present section.

The declarations must also indicate which taxes are subject to abatement and the communes in which said taxes are levied.

All declarations shall be received during the first three months of each year, and shall be valid as long as the information which they contain remains correct; when the information ceases to be correct, the declarations must be reviewed within the above-stated period.

SEC. 53. The income from mining operations and from such transactions as are grouped with them in the assessment of proportional mining royalties shall remain subject to such royalties, in accordance with existing laws, and shall not be subject to the taxes created by this act.

SEC. 54. Total or partial omissions in the assessment of any of the taxes created by the present act may, if proved, be made good any time before the expiration of the fifth year following that as to which the incomplete assessment was made.

SEC. 55. For the purpose of assessing the divers income taxes, the administration of direct taxes shall be entitled to require all public offices to communicate the data collected by them under existing laws.

EXCESS-PROFITS TAX

SYNOPSIS OF EXCESS-PROFITS TAX LAWS OF VARIOUS COUNTRIES.

A. ALLIED COUNTRIES.

GREAT BRITAIN. Finance (No. 2) Act, 1915 (5 and 6 Geo. 5, c. 89), Part III, as amended by Finance Act, 1916 (6 and 7 Geo. 5, c. 24), Part III, and Finance Act, 1917 (7 and 8 Geo 5, c. 31), Part III.

Basis of tax.—Excess of profits during war trade years over prewar standard; prewar standard being the average of any two of the last three prewar trade years selected by the taxpayer, except that it is not to be counted at less than 6 per cent (in the case of businesses not carried on by a company or corporation, 8 per cent) on the capital invested at the end of the last prewar-trade year. Allowance is made for increase in capital during a war trade year at the rate of 9 per cent (in the case of noncorporate businesses, 11 per cent); for decrease in capital during a war trade year, at the rate of 6 per cent (for noncorporate businesses, 7 per cent). If the average profits of the last three prewar years were 25 per cent or more lower than during the three previous years, any four of the six years may be taken as a basis for the prewar standard. In the case of new businesses, the prewar standard is counted as 9 per cent of the capital invested (or for noncorporate business, 11 per cent).

Exemptions—(1) Amount: £200, increased by one-fifth of the amount by which the profits are less than £2,000 if the prewar standard does not exceed £500. (2) Kinds of business: Agriculture, offices, professions, insolvent businesses in the hands of a liquidator.

Rate of tax.—80 per cent.

CANADA. Business Profits War Tax Act, 1916 (6 and 7 Geo. 5, c. 11), as amended by act of July 25, 1917 (7 and 8 Geo. 5, c. 6), and by the act which, as bill 84, had its first reading in the House of Commons May 8, 1918.

Basis of tax.—Excess of profits over 7 per cent of the capital (in the case of businesses not carried on by a company or corporation, 10 per cent).

Exemptions.—(1) Amount: Excess profits on a capital of less than $25,000, except in the case of munition makers and dealers in war supplies and materials. (2) Kinds of business: Life insurance, agriculture, provincial or municipal business undertakings.

Rate of tax.—	Per cent.
Where the capital is less than $50,000	25
Where the capital is more than $50,000:	
On the taxable portion of profits which are not more than 15 per cent of the capital	25
On the portion between 15 per cent and 20 per cent	50
On the portion in excess of 20 per cent	75

AUSTRALIA. War-time Profits Tax Assessment Act, 1917, and War-time Profits Tax Act, 1917.

Basis of tax.—The excess of profits during war trade years over prewar standard of profits, prewar standard being the average of any two of the last three prewar trade years selected by the taxpayer, except that it is not to be counted as less than £500. Allowance is made for increase or decrease of capital during a war trade year at the rate of 10 per cent. If the average profits of the last three prewar years were 25 per cent, or more, lower than during the three preceding years, any two of the three earlier years may be substituted by the taxpayer. Whenever the prewar standard exceeds £500, the exemption of £200 (see below) is reduced by one-fourth of the amount of excess profits above £200. In the case of new businesses, the prewar standard is counted, at the option of the taxpayer, at 10 per cent of the capital invested, or at the actual prewar profits, reckoned on a yearly basis, or at the amount of the taxpayer's income from his previous occupation

Exemptions.—(1) Amount £200. (2) Kinds of business (*a*) Public or philanthropic enterprises, and life insurance; (*b*) the production, manufacture, or distribution of native foodstuffs; (*c*) offices, (*d*) professions, (*e*) gold mines, (*f*) certain industries connected with munition making (3) Class of persons Owners of, or partners in, taxable enterprises, who are in active military service

Rate of tax.—75 per cent.

NEW ZEALAND. The excess-profits tax imposed by Part II of the Finance Act, 1916 (7 Geo. 5, No. 7), was abolished in the budget for 1917-18 and additional taxation on land and incomes was substituted. (Board of Trade Journal, v. 99, p. 141, Oct. 18, 1917.) The following refers to the tax of 1916

Basis of tax.—Excess of personal income for war income years over (1) income for any one (or the average of any two or of all) of the three income years prior to March 31, 1914; or (2) 7½ per cent on the capital employed by the taxpayer in producing his income, plus a sum not over £600 as remuneration for personal exertion, at the election of the taxpayer. Allowance for increase or decrease in capital since the year or years taken as the prewar standard is made at the rate of 7½ per cent. Allowance may also be made for net loss in any business for the aggregate period of three years ending March 31, 1915 In no case is the standard from which the "excess" income is to be measured to be counted as less than £300.

Exemptions.—(1) Amount £300 taxable income. (2) Kind of income: Salaries and wages.

Rate of tax.—45 per cent.

UNION OF SOUTH AFRICA. Income Tax (Consolidation) Act, 1917, Chap. IV. (Union Gazette Extraordinary, July 21, 1917, pp. xxv-xxxi.)

Basis of tax.—Excess of profits during war trade years over prewar standard of profits; prewar standard being the last prewar trade year, except that it is not to be counted as less than 8 per cent (in the case of businesses not carried on by a corporation, 10 per cent) on the capital invested. Allowance is made for increase or decrease of capital at a rate equal to the percentage which the prewar profits bore to the prewar capital. In cases in which the average profits of the last prewar trade year were at least 25 per cent lower than the combined average of that year and the two years preceding, the average profits of all three years is the standard. In the case of new businesses the prewar standard is 8 per cent (in the case of businesses not carried on by a corporation, 10 per cent) of the capital.

Exemptions.—(1) Amount: (*a*) £500; (*b*) amount whereby profits for any preceding war trade year have fallen below prewar standard. (2) Kinds of business: Gold mining, noncorporate diamond mining, life insurance, offices, investments, professions.

Rate of tax.—25 per cent.

BRITISH GUIANA. Tax ordinance, 1918 (No. 24 of 1917), as summarized in the Board of Trade Journal (Great Britain), March 14, 1918, p. 306.

Basis of tax.—Profits in excess of 10 per cent on the capital invested.

Exemptions.—(1) Amount: Profits where the capital is less than $5,000. (2) Kinds of business: Fire and life insurance, shipping, cable, building, and benevolent societies.

Rate of tax.—10 per cent. But in the case of banking institutions a fixed tax of $1,500 a year is substituted for the percentage rate; and where the amount of capital employed or the profits earned in the colony by any business can not be satisfactorily arrived at, the rate is 2 per cent of the total amount of sales, purchases, and commissions of such business in the colony.

FRANCE. Law of July 1, 1916, as amended by section 8 of the law of December 30, 1916, and sections 4 to 8 of the law of December 31, 1917.

Basis of tax.—Excess of profits during war trade years over prewar standard of profits; prewar standard being the average of the last three years prior to August 1, 1914, but not to be counted as less than 5,000 francs nor less than 8 per cent on the capital invested.

Exemptions.—(1) Amount: In the case of mine owners and persons subject to the business-license tax, 5,000 francs; in the case of plants wrecked by the war or located in the invaded territory, 6 per cent of the capital invested; in the case of all who are subject to the tax, extra amounts necessary for depreciation. (2) Kinds of business: All except those conducted by mine owners, persons subject to a business-license tax, and persons furnishing supplies to the Government.

Rate of tax—	Per cent.
On the portion of the taxable profits below 100,000 francs	50
On the portion between 100,000 francs and 250,000 francs	60
On the portion between 250,000 francs and 500,000 francs	70
On the portion exceeding 500,000 francs	80

TUNIS. Beylical decree of September 20, 1917. (Board of Trade Journal, November 15, 1917, p. 363.)

Basis of tax.—(1) New or exceptional profits realized in consequence of the war; (2) all profits realized during war years in excess of the average for the two prewar years. The tax is payable in installments and extends over a period ending one year after the termination of hostilities.

Exemptions.—(1) Amount: (*a*) 5,000 francs; (*b*) as to mining companies, that portion of the tax equal to the tax paid by them under a decree of December 29, 1913. (2) Kinds of business: A list of occupations exempted is annexed to the decree

Rate of tax.—50 per cent on taxable profits not more than 500,000 francs; 60 per cent on those above 500,000 francs.

ITALY. Decrees of November 21, December 23, 1915, Nos 1643, 1893, February 17, August 6, August 31, October 1, November 9, November 19, 1916, Nos. 243, 1039, 1090, 1345, 1525, 1568; January 18, May 24, June 14, October 1, November 29, 1917, Nos. 145, 894, 971, 1562, 1934 Regulations of the ministry of finance, January 15, 1916. (Collezione celerifera delle leggi, decreti, etc., 1915, p. 1532; 1916, pp 91, 100, 307, 833, 861, 1091, 1187, 1296; 1917, pp. 168, 529, 562, 891, 1116.)

Basis of tax.—New profits or excess of profits during war-trade years over the average of the amounts ascertained for personal-property tax for the years 1913 and 1914; but this average is not to be counted as less than 8 per cent on the capital invested

Exemptions.—(1) Amount, 2,500 lire or less; in the case of commission agents, 10 per cent increase in income or less. (2) Kind of business: (*a*) The tax is imposed only on merchants and manufacturers, and on commission agents; (*b*) those helping to advance the Italian mercantile marine enjoy a qualified exemption.

Rates of tax.—	Per cent.
(1) For merchants and manufacturers:	
On fraction of profits from 8 to 10 per cent on capital invested	20
On fraction of profits from 10 to 15 per cent on capital invested	30
On fraction of profits from 15 to 20 per cent on capital invested	40
On fraction of profits over 20 per cent on capital invested	60
(2) For commission agents:	
On excess over 10 per cent up to 50 per cent of prewar profits	10
On excess over 50 per cent up to 100 per cent of prewar profits	15
On excess over 100 per cent up to 200 per cent of prewar profits	20
On excess over 200 per cent up to 300 per cent of prewar profits	25
On excess over 300 per cent of prewar profits	40

RUSSIA. Decree of May 13/26, 1916 (Bulletin of the Government orders relating to the ministry of finance and the ministry of commerce and industry, No. 21, May 22/June 4, 1916, pp. 386–389), as amended by decree of the Provisional Government, June 12/25, 1917 (summarized in the Board of Trade Journal (Great Britain), Oct. 4, 1917, p. 26).

Basis of tax.—Excess of profits or remuneration received during a war trade year over prewar standard; prewar standard being the profits or remuneration received in 1913 and/or 1914, except that in the case of companies also subject to the supplementary industrial tax on total profits, such prewar standard is not to be counted as less than 6 per cent of the capital. In the case of new enterprises, the prewar standard is, for companies subject to the supplementary industrial tax, 6 per cent of the capital, and for other companies or persons, one-fourth of the profits or remuneration received in 1916, except that in the case of commercial intermediaries doing business without special premises, the prewar standard is zero.

Exemptions.—(1) Amount: (*a*) In the case of companies subject to the supplementary industrial tax, the amount whereby the sum of that tax, their income tax and their excess profits tax exceeds 90 per cent of their income; (*b*) in the case of other profit-making concerns or occupations, excess profits of less than 500 roubles. or excess profits where the total profits are less than 2,000 roubles; (*c*) in the case of directors, managers, etc , excess remuneration of less than 500 roubles; (*d*) in the case of commercial intermediaries. total profits if their 1916 profits were less than 3,000 roubles. (2) Kinds of business: The tax affects all who profit directly or indirectly from commercial transactions, including directors, managers, etc

Rate of tax.—As to enterprises also subject to the supplementary industrial tax, from 40 per cent on profits amounting to 6 per cent of the capital, to 80 per cent on profits amounting to 20 per cent of the capital; as to other undertakings and persons, from 30 per cent on the amount of excess profits or remuneration less than 1,000 roubles to 60 per cent on the amount which exceeds 100,000.

JAPAN. Budget bill, 1918–19 (summarized and explained by Finance Minister Shoda before the Imperial Diet, Jan. 22, 1918, cf New York Evening Post, Japan Number, March 16. 1918, pp. 44–45)

Basis of tax —Excess of profit during war-trade year over prewar standard; prewar standard being for corporations the average profit of [any] two prewar trade years, for individuals the average profit of the two years preceding 1914. The tax is to be abolished the year of the restoration of peace.

Exemptions.—20 per cent of the prewar standard of profits.

Rate of tax.—On corporations, 20 per cent: on individuals, 15 per cent.

B. CENTRAL POWERS.

GERMANY. Law of June 21, 1916 (Reichsgesetzblatt, 1916, pp. 561–572), as amended by law of December 17, 1916 (ibid., 1916, p. 1407), and law of April 9, 1917 (ibid., 1916, pp. 349–350).

1. PROPERTY INCREASE TAX (INDIVIDUALS).

Basis of tax.—Any increase in the total value of the property of individuals between January 1, 1914, and December 31, 1916, excluding all increases due to transfer of property at death or *inter vivos*.

Exemptions.—(1) Any increase of not more than 3,000 marks; (2) any increase where the total amount of the increased value of the property is not more than 10,000 marks; (3) that portion of any increase equal to the difference between the original capital and 10,000 marks, whenever the total amount of the increased capital is not more than 15,000 marks.

Rate of tax.—

Property increase.	Tax.	Surtax.
	Per cent.	*Per cent.*
On the first 10,000 marks	5	1
On the next 10,000 marks or fraction thereof	10	2
On the next 10,000 marks or fraction thereof	15	3
On the next 20,000 marks or fraction thereof	20	4
On the next 50,000 marks or fraction thereof	25	5
On the next 100,000 marks or fraction thereof	30	6
On the next 200,000 marks or fraction thereof	35	7
On the next 300,000 marks or fraction thereof	40	8
On the next 300,000 marks or fraction thereof	45	9
On any further amount	50	10

If the increased capital of a taxable individual does not exceed 100,000 marks, he receives an abatement—

If he has 3 children under 18 of one-fourth the amount of the surtax.
If he has 4 children under 18 of one-half the amount of the surtax.
If he has 5 children under 18 of three-fourths the amount of the surtax.
If he has more than 5 children under 18 the whole of the surtax.

2. EXCESS-PROFITS TAX (BUSINESS COMPANIES).

Basis of tax.—Excess of profits of domestic and foreign companies during war-trade years over prewar standard of profits; prewar standard being the average of those three of the last five prewar years arrived at by excluding the year with the largest and the year with the smallest profits, if company has existed for five years, except that it is not to be counted as less than 6 per cent on the paid-up original capital stock.

Exemptions.—5,000 marks.
Rate of tax.—

A. DOMESTIC COMPANIES.

TAX.

If ratio of average annual excess profits to capital stock and reserve amounts to—	Rate of tax on excess profits.
	Per cent.
Not more than 2 per cent	10
More than 2 per cent, but not more than 5 per cent	15
More than 5 per cent, but not more than 10 per cent	20
More than 10 per cent, but not more than 15 per cent	25
More than 15 per cent	30

SURTAX.

If ratio of average annual total profits during war trade years to capital stock and reserve amounts to—	Rate of surtax percentage of principal tax.
	Per cent.
More than 8 per cent, but not more than 10 per cent	10
More than 10 per cent, but not more than 15 per cent	20
More than 15 per cent, but not more than 20 per cent	30
More than 20 per cent, but not more than 25 per cent	40
More than 25 per cent	50

B.—FOREIGN COMPANIES.

If excess profits amount to—	Rate of tax on excess profits.
	Per cent.
Not more than 20,000 marks	10
More than 20,000 marks but not more than 40,000 marks	12
More than 40,000 marks but not more than 60,000 marks	14
More than 60,000 marks but not more than 80,000 marks	16
More than 80,000 marks but not more than 100,000 marks	18
More than 100,000 marks but not more than 120,000 marks	20
More than 120,000 marks but not more than 140,000 marks	22
More than 140,000 marks but not more than 160,000 marks	24
More than 160,000 marks but not more than 180,000 marks	26
More than 180,000 marks but not more than 200,000 marks	28
More than 200,000 marks but not more than 250,000 marks	30
More than 250,000 marks but not more than 500,000 marks	40
More than 500,000 marks	45

Rate of tax on domestic and foreign companies proposed in place of the above rates by the budget bill 1918–19 (Board of Trade Journal, May 23, 1918, p. 654, citing the Deutscher Reichsanzeiger)

If excess profits amount to—	Or (in the case of German companies whose excess profits do not exceed 1,000,000 marks) if the ratio of total profits to capital stock and reserve amounts to—	Rate of tax.
		Per cent.
Less than 50,000 marks	Less than 8 per cent	30
Less than 100,000 marks	Less than 10 per cent	36
Less than 200,000 marks	Less than 15 per cent	42
Less than 300,000 marks	Less than 20 per cent	48
Less than 500,000 marks	Less than 25 per cent	54
500,000 marks or more	25 per cent or more	60

AUSTRIA. Decree of April 16, 1916; Regulations of minister of finance of August 8, 1916. There are two separate taxes—on the excess profits of business companies and on the income increase of individuals (R. G. Bl. 1916, No. 103, 247.)

1. EXCESS-PROFITS TAX (BUSINESS COMPANIES).

Basis of tax.—Excess of profits during war trade-years over prewar standard of profits; prewar standard being the average of the five trade-years prior to August 1, 1914, excluding the maximum and the minimum of these years, if the company has been in existence five years, otherwise the average of the last three prewar trade-years; but in no case is the prewar standard to be taken as less than 6 per cent on the capital invested. Allowance for increase of capital is made at the rate of 6 per cent.

Exemptions.—Excess profits of 10,000 kroner or less.

Rates of tax—

(1) Domestic companies:

On portion of excess profits not over 5 per cent on capital invested, 10 per cent.

On portion of excess profits over 5 per cent but not over 10 per cent on capital invested, 15 per cent.

On portion of excess profits over 10 per cent but not over 15 per cent on capital invested, 20 per cent.

On portion of excess profits over 15 per cent but not over 20 per cent on capital invested, 25 per cent.

On portion of excess profits over 20 per cent but not over 25 per cent on capital invested, 30 per cent.

On portion of excess profits over 25 per cent on capital invested, 35 per cent.

(2) Foreign companies:

On excess profits of not more than 200,000 kroner, 20 per cent.

On excess profits of more than 200,000 but not more than 400,000 kroner, 25 per cent.

On excess profits of more than 400,000 but not more than 700,000 kroner, 30 per cent.

On excess profits of more than 700,000 but not more than 1,000,000 kroner, 35 per cent.

On excess profits of more than 1,000,000 kroner, 40 per cent.

2. INCOME INCREASE TAX (INDIVIDUALS).

Basis of tax.—Excess of income during war years over income for 1913 or at the option of the taxpayer the average income for 1911, 1912, and 1913; but the prewar income not to be counted as less than 10,000 kroner.

Exemptions.—(1) Amount: 3,000 kroner or less. (2) Kinds of income: Salaries, wages, and pensions paid from public funds, or from other sources if not over 4,000 kroner.

Rate of tax—

On the first 10,000 kroner of income increase, 5 per cent.

On the next 10,000 kroner of income increase, 10 per cent.

On the next 20,000 kroner of income increase, 15 per cent.

On the next 20,000 kroner of income increase, 20 per cent.

On the next 20,000 kroner of income increase, 25 per cent.

On the next 20,000 kroner of income increase, 30 per cent.

On the next 200,000 kroner of income increase, 35 per cent.

On the next 200,000 kroner of income increase, 40 per cent.

On any further amount of income increase, 45 per cent.

HUNGARY. According to an announcement of a new taxation system, July 2, 1916 (Information Annual, 1916, p. 36):

The war-profit tax was to be arranged on a rising scale, whereby corporations must pay in proportion to their increased profits in relation to capitalization if the business was local. If the profit accrued from a business in a foreign country, it must pay 20 per cent of profits up to 200,000 kronen; 25 per cent of profits between 200,000 and 400,000 kronen; 30 per cent of war profits between 400,000 and 700,000 kronen; 35 per cent of profits from that point up to a million kronen; and 40 per cent of all profits over that figure. For individuals the war-profit tax would begin with a levy of 5 per cent on excess profits up to 10,000 kronen, and continue to 45 per cent on 500,000 kronen.

BULGARIA. Proposed tax on total war profits, according to a Government bill laid before the Sobranje the end of 1917. (London Economist, Dec. 8, 1917; New York Journal of Commerce, Jan. 2, 1918.)

Basis of tax.—Aggregate profits for the entire period of the war.

Exemptions.—(1) Amount: 5,000 leva. (2) Kinds of business: Among others, agriculture.

Rate of tax—

Amount of taxable profit	Rate on Government contracts.	Rate on other business.
	Per cent.	*Per cent.*
Less than 50,000 leva	55	40
50,000 to 100,000 leva	50	35
More than 100,000 leva	45	30

C. NEUTRAL COUNTRIES.

NETHERLANDS. Law of June 22, 1916. (Staatsblad van het Koninkrijk der landen, 1916, No. 268.)

Basis of tax.—Increased income or profits during war years over the average for the years 1911, 1912, and 1913; income of companies not to be counted as less than 5 per cent on the capital invested. Allowance for increase in capital is made at the rate of 5 per cent. The tax is computed only for income increase resulting directly or indirectly from the state of war.

Exemptions.—(1) Amount: Income increase of 1,000 florins. (2) Kind of income: Salaries and wages paid up by quasi public corporations; salaries or wages paid in pursuance of a labor contract.

Rate of tax.—On increase of less than 2,500 florins with deduction of 1,000 florins, 10 per cent. On increase of 2,500 florins or over, with deduction of 2,000 florins, 30 per cent.

DENMARK. Law of May 10, 1915 (Samling af Love, 1915A, p. 298), as amended by law of May 17, 1916 (ibid., 1916A, p. 896), and law of May 14, 1917 (ibid., 1917A, p. 461).

1. TAX ON INCOME INCREASE OF INDIVIDUALS.

Basis of tax.—Excess of income for war year over average income of highest two of the three years 1912–13, 1913–14, 1914–15.

Exemptions.—(1) Amount: 6,000 crowns. (2) Kinds of incomes: Annuities, endowments, lottery winnings, insurance money, part of inheritances.

Rate of tax.—The tax is graduated both according to amount of income and amount of income increase, varying from 1 per cent on the smallest amounts to 30 per cent on incomes of a million crowns or more.

2. TAX ON EXCESS PROFITS OF CORPORATIONS OR STOCK COMPANIES.

Basis of tax.—Excess of profits during war trade years over prewar standard of profits; prewar standard being the average of the two of the three trade years 1912–13, 1913–14, 1914–15, in which the largest profits were made, except that it is not to be counted as less than 5 per cent on the capital invested. Allowance for increase of capital is made at the rate of 6 per cent.

Exemptions.—(1) Amount: 5 per cent or less on the paid-up capital. (2) Kinds of corporations: Charitable corporations, coöperative societies, mutual liability insurance companies.

Rate of tax—

Ratio of income to capital invested.	Rate of tax.
	Per cent.
Less than 8 per cent	8
More than 8 per cent, but less than 10 per cent	10
More than 10 per cent, but less than 15 per cent	12
More than 15 per cent, but less than 20 per cent	15
More than 20 per cent, but less than 25 per cent	20
More than 25 per cent, but less than 30 per cent	25
More than 30 per cent, but less than 40 per cent	26
More than 40 per cent, but less than 50 per cent	27
More than 50 per cent, but less than 75 per cent	28
More than 75 per cent, but less than 100 per cent	29
More than 100 per cent	30

In the case of companies with a capital of less than 50,000 crowns, or of new companies, the minimum tax is 10 per cent

3. WAR TAX SUPPLEMENTARY TO THE ORDINARY INCOME AND PROPERTY TAX

Basis of tax.—The same as in the case of the ordinary income and property tax imposed by the law of June 8, 1912 It consists of two taxes, the one levied on the taxpayer's entire property, the other on his entire income

Exemptions —(1) Amount: (*a*) as to the tax on property, property worth less than 24,000 crowns, or property of a man having an income of less than 2,000; (*b*) as to the tax on incomes, incomes of less than 8,000 (2) Kinds of income. The same as are exempted in the law of June 8, 1912 (3) Special exemption. When the amount of this tax is less than the amount of the tax on the income increase of the same individual; if, on the other hand, the amount of his income increase tax is less, he is exempt from payment of that tax.

Rate of tax.—(*a*) as to property, graduated from 0.01 per cent on the smallest amounts to 0.125 on property valued at over one million. (*b*) as to income, graduated from 0.1 per cent on the lowest incomes to 4.5 per cent on incomes of over 100,000

NORWAY. Law of August 17, 1915 (Norge lovtidende 1915 (2), p. 699), as amended by law of February 23, 1916 (ibid., 1916 (2), p. 52), and law of May 4, 1917 (ibid , 1917 (2), p. 236) Proclamations of February 25, 1916 (ibid., 1916 (2), p 56), and May 14, 1917 (ibid., 1917 (2), p. 267)

Basis of tax.—Excess of income during war-trade years over prewar standard; prewar standard being the average for the two years 1912–13 and 1913–14 (in the case of companies, 1912 and 1913). In case there was no income assessment for either of these years, the income for 1916 is taken instead.

Exemptions.—(1) Amount Incomes assessed at less than 10,000 kroner; income increase of less than 2,000 kroner (2) Kinds of income: (*a*) income increase not due to the European war; (*b*) income from sources other than shipping fishing, or mining.

Rate of tax.—

Taxable portion of excess income	Per cent.
Less than 5,000 crowns	5
Between 5,000 and 15,000 crowns	7½
Between 15,000 and 30,000 crowns	10
Between 30,000 and 50,000 crowns	12½
Between 50,000 and 75,000 crowns	15
Between 75,000 and 100,000 crowns	17½
Between 100,000 and 150,000 crowns	20
Between 150,000 and 200,000 crowns	25
More than 200,000 crowns	30

SWEDEN. Decree of June 11, 1915 (Svensk forfattnings-samling, 1915, No. 210), as amended by decree of June 30, 1916 (ibid., 1916, No. 260).

Basis of tax —Increased incomes of individuals or companies during war years over average income for 1913 and 1914.

Exemptions —(1) Amount. Excess income of less than 2,000 crowns; excess income where the entire income is less than 10,000 crowns; excess income of companies where the entire income is less than 5 per cent of the capital. (2) Kinds of income: (*a*) Any as to which the increase can be proved to be not the result of war conditions; incomes of employees, servants, and pension holders.

Rate of tax.—

Excess income in crowns.	Rate.	Increased rate for each full 100 crowns falling between figure in column 1 and next higher figure.
	Per cent.	*Per cent.*
2,000	12	13
20,000	13	15
40,000	14	17
60,000	15	19
80,000	16	21
100,000	17	20
150,000	18	22
200,000	19	24
250,000	20	26
300,000	21	28
350,000	22	30
400,000	23	32
450,000	24	34
500,000 or over	25	.....

SPAIN. Tax law proposed in connection with 1917 budget, June 4, 1916; royal decree of June 23, 1916. (Gaceta de Madrid, No. 156, p. 542; No. 175, p. 729, U. S. Commerce Reports, Aug. 14, 1916, p. 581.)

Basis of tax.—Excess of profits over 7 per cent on capital invested.

Rate of tax.—

On that portion of profits not over 20 per cent on the capital invested, 25 per cent.

On that portion of profits over 20 per cent but not over 35 per cent on the capital invested, 30 per cent.

On that portion of profits over 35 per cent but not over 50 per cent on the capital invested, 35 per cent.

On that portion of profits over 50 per cent on the capital invested, 40 per cent.

SWITZERLAND. Decree of the federal council, September 18, 1916 (Recueil officiel, 1916, p. 355), as amended by decree of February 9, 1917 (Schweizerische Gesetzsammlung, 1917, p. 59).

Basis of tax.—(1) In the case of regular businesses established in Switzerland: The excess of profits during war-trade years over prewar standard of profits; prewar standard being the average of the two last prewar commercial years, except that it is not to be counted as less than 5,000 francs, nor, in the case of corporations, as less than 5 per cent of the capital stock. Allowances are made for increased capital at the rate of 5 per cent. For new businesses, including newly established Swiss branches of foreign businesses, the prewar standard is 5 per cent of the capital stock.

(2) In the case of isolated business transactions, including all transactions conducted by individuals or corporations having no permanent establishment in Switzerland. The entire profits, without deduction.

Exemptions.—(1) Amount, (*a*) 10,000 francs (which is raised to 15,000 in the case of joint-stock companies (*commandites*) and to 20,000 where these have more than two members); (*b*) excess profits equal to 10 per cent of the prewar standard of profits. (2) Kinds of profits: Those arising from noncommercial transactions.

Rate of tax.—25 per cent.

GREAT BRITAIN.

EXCESS-PROFITS DUTY, 1915–1918.

FINANCE (NO. 2) ACT, 1915.

[5 and 6 Geo V, c. 89.]

PART II.

INCOME TAX AND EXCESS-PROFITS DUTY.

35. (1) Where any person has paid excess-profits duty under this act the amount so paid shall be allowed as a deduction for the purpose of income tax in computing the profits and gains of the year which included the end of the accounting period in respect of which the excess-profits duty has been paid; but where any person has received repayment of any amount previously paid by him by way of excess-profits duty, the amount repaid shall be treated as profit for the year in which the repayment is received.

The payment of excess-profits duty shall not be deemed to be a specific cause for the purposes of section 134 of the Income Tax Act, 1842.

(2) Where in any income tax year the profits or gains from which a deduction may be made under this section come into computation, but owing to the time at which the amount of excess-profits duty became ascertained it was impracticable to give effect to the deduction when assessing income tax, the amount by which the income tax would have been reduced if effect had been given to the deduction shall be deducted from the amount payable for excess-profits duty, or if there is no excess-profits duty, shall be repaid to the taxpayer

*   *   *   *   *   *   *

PART III.

EXCESS-PROFITS DUTY.

RATE OF DUTY.

38. (1) There shall be charged, levied, and paid on the amount by which the profits arising from any trade or business to which this part of this act applies, in any accounting period which ended after

the 4th day of August, 1914, and before the 1st day of July, 1915, exceeded, by more than £200, the prewar standard of profits as defined for the purposes of this part of this act, a duty (in this act referred to as "excess-profits duty") of an amount equal to 50 per cent of that excess.[1]

ACCOUNTING PERIOD.

(2) For the purposes of this part of this act the accounting period shall be taken to be the period for which the accounts of the trade or business have been made up, and where the accounts of any trade or business have not been made up for any definite period, or for the period for which they have been usually made up, or a year or more has elapsed without accounts being made up, shall be taken to be such period not being less than six months or more than a year ending on such a date as the commissioners of inland revenue may determine.

Where any accounting period is a period of less than a year this section shall have effect as if there were substituted for £200 a proportionately reduced amount.

(3) Where a person proves that in any accounting period which ended after the 4th day of August, 1914, his profits have not reached the point which involves liability to excess-profits duty, or that he has sustained a loss in his trade or business, he shall be entitled to repayment of such amount paid by him as excess-profits duty in respect of any previous accounting period, or to set off against any excess-profits duty payable by him in respect of any succeeding accounting period such an amount as will make the total amount of excess-profits duty paid by him during the whole period accord with his profits or losses during that period.

TRADES AND BUSINESSES TO WHICH DUTY APPLIES.

39. The trades and businesses to which this part of this act applies are all trades or businesses (whether continuously carried on or not) of any description carried on in the United Kingdom, or owned or carried on in any other place by persons ordinarily resident in the United Kingdom, excepting—

(*a*) Husbandry in the United Kingdom; and

(*b*) Offices or employments; and

(*c*) Any profession the profits of which are dependent mainly on the personal qualifications of the person by whom the profession is carried on and in which no capital expenditure is required, or only capital expenditure of a comparatively small amount—

but including the business of any person taking commissions in respect of any transactions or services rendered, and of any agent of any description (not being a commercial traveler, or an agent whose remuneration consists wholly of a fixed and definite sum not depending on the amount of business done or any other contingency).

[1] Rate of duty increased to 60 per cent by Finance Act, 1916, sec. 45 (2) and to 80 per cent by Finance Act, 1917, sec. 20. Exemption limit raised in certain cases by Finance Act, 1917, sec. 26 (4), *v. infra.*

DETERMINATION OF PROFITS AND PREWAR STANDARD.

40. (1) The profits arising from any trade or business to which this part of this act applies shall be separately determined for the purpose of this part of this act, but shall be so determined on the same principles as the profits and gains of the trade or business are or would be determined for the purpose of income tax, subject to the modifications set out in the first part of the Fourth Schedule to this act and to any other provisions of this act.

(2) The prewar standard of profits for the purposes of this part of this act shall, subject to the provisions of this act, be taken to be the amount of the profits arising from the trade or business on the average of any two of the three last prewar trade years, to be selected by the taxpayer (in this part of this act referred to as the profits standard): *Provided*, That if it is shown to the satisfaction of the commissioners of inland revenue that that amount was less than the percentage standard as hereinafter defined, the prewar standard of profits shall be taken to be the percentage standard.

The percentage standard shall, for the purposes of this part of this act, be taken to be an amount equal to the statutory percentage on the capital of the trade or business as existing at the end of the last prewar trade year, subject, however, to the provisions of this act as to any alteration in the manner of calculating the percentage standard in special cases.

The statutory percentage shall be 6 per cent in the case of a trade or business carried on or owned by a company or other body corporate, and 7 per cent[1] in the case of any other trade or business, subject, however, to the provisions of this act as to the increase in that percentage in certain cases.

The provisions contained in the second part of the Fourth Schedule to this act shall have effect with respect to the computation of the profits of a prewar trade year, and the provisions contained in the third part of the Fourth Schedule shall have effect with respect to the ascertainment of capital for the purposes of this part of this act.

"The last prewar trade year" means the year ending at the end of the last accounting period before the 5th day of August, 1914, and "the three last prewar trade years" means the three years ending at the three corresponding times.

(3) Where it appears to the commissioners of inland revenue, on the application of a taxpayer in any particular case, that any provisions of the Fourth Schedule to this act should be modified in his case, owing to a change in the constitution of a partnership, or to the postponement or suspension, as a consequence of the present war, of renewals or repairs, or to exceptional depreciation or obsolescence of assets employed in the trade or business due to the present war, or to the necessity in connection with the present war of providing plant which will not be wanted for the purposes of the trade or business after the termination of the war, or to any other special circumstances specified in regulations made by the Treasury, those commissioners shall have power to allow such modifications of any of the provisions of that schedule as they think necessary in order to meet the particular case.

[1] Increased to 8 per cent by Finance Act, 1917, sec. 26 (2).

If the commissioners refuse, on any such application, to allow any modification, or if the applicant is dissatisfied with any modification allowed, the applicant may require the commissioners to refer the case to a board of referees, to be appointed for the purposes of this part of this act by the Treasury,[1] and that board shall consider any case so referred and have the same powers with respect thereto as the commissioners have.

ADJUSTMENTS FOR INCREASED OR DECREASED CAPITAL.

41. (1) Where capital has been increased during the accounting period, a deduction shall be made from the profits of the accounting period at the statutory percentage[2] per annum on the amount by which the capital has been increased for the whole accounting period, if the increased capital has been employed for the whole accounting period; and if the increased capital has been employed for part only of the accounting period, for that part of the accounting period.

(2) Where capital has been decreased during the accounting period, an addition shall be made to the profits of the accounting period at the statutory percentage per annum on the amount by which the capital has been so decreased for the whole accounting period, if the capital has been decreased for the whole accounting period; and if the capital has been decreased for part only of the accounting period, for that part of the accounting period.

(3) For the purposes of this section capital shall be taken to be increased or decreased, as the case may be, where the prewar standard of profits is a profits standard, if the capital employed in the trade or business exceeds or is less than the average amount of capital employed during the prewar trade years or year by reference to which the profits standard has been arrived at; and, where the prewar standard of profits is a percentage standard, if the capital exceeds or is less than the capital on which the percentage standard has been calculated.

(4) Where any capital employed in a trade or business which was so employed for the first time within three years[3] before the 1st day of August, 1914, has only commenced to be remunerative, or fully remunerative, in the accounting period, an amount equal to the statutory percentage, or where interest has been earned on the capital, but at a rate less than the statutory percentage, an amount which would bring the interest earned on the capital up to the statutory percentage, as the case may be, shall be added to the profits standard.

BOARD OF REFEREES—INCREASE OF PERCENTAGES, ETC.

42. Where an application is made to the commissioners of inland revenue—

(1) For an increase of the statutory percentage as respects any class of trade or business, or for a calculation of the percentage standard in the case of any class of trade or business in which the amount of capital actually employed in the trade or business is, owing to the

[1] Amended by Finance Act, 1916, sec. 55 to provide that in the case of controlled establishments the minister of munitions shall appoint the referees, *v. infra*.
[2] Three per cent added to this by Finance Act, 1917, sec. 26 (1), *v. infra*.
[3] Changed to six years by Finance Act, 1917, sec. 26 (7), *v. infra*.

nature of the trade or business, small compared with the capital necessarily at stake for that trade or business, by reference to some factor other than the capital of the trade or business or to some additional factor: or

(2) For an alteration of the prewar standard of profits as respects capital employed for the purpose of the manufacture of war materials or for munitions work and which could not be expected to be remunerative, or wholly remunerative, except in time of war, in a business which has been wholly or mainly carried on for those purposes—

the commissioners, unless they are of opinion that the application is frivolous or vexatious or relates to matters already decided by a board of referees, shall refer the case to a board of referees to be appointed for the purpose of this part of this act by the Treasury, and that board shall deal with the case, and may, by order, if they think fit, increase the statutory percentage or alter the percentage standard for the class of trade or business the subject of the order, or alter the prewar standard of profits, as the case requires.

On any such order being made, this part of this act shall have effect as from the date named in the order as if the percentage or standard named in the order was substituted for the percentage or standard fixed by this act; and where, in pursuance of any such order, the statutory percentage is increased or the percentage standard is altered as respects any class of trade or business, the statutory percentage shall be increased and the percentage standard shall be altered, respectively, for all purposes of this part of this act as respects any trade or business belonging to that class.

This section shall apply to any subdivision of a trade or business based either on any special feature of the trade or business or on locality as it applies to a class of trade or business, in any case where the board of referees are of opinion that the subdivision can properly be dealt with separately.

EXCESS MINERAL RIGHTS DUTY.

43. (1) Where the amount payable to any person as rent in respect of the right to work minerals or of any mineral wayleaves (in cases where the right to work the minerals and the mineral wayleaves are not part of the assets of any trade or business) varies according to the price of the minerals, and the amount so payable in respect of any working year ending on any date after the commencement of the present war (in this section referred to as the accounting year) exceeds the prewar standard of that rent, there shall be paid as in addition to any mineral rights duty payable or paid, either directly or by deduction, by reference to the amount of the rent paid in that working year, by that person (in this section referred to as the person liable) an amount equal to 50 per cent of that excess.[1]

(2) The prewar standard of rent shall, for the purposes of this section, be taken to be the average of any two of the three last prewar rent values, to be selected by the taxpayer, and in cases where the minerals have not been worked or the wayleaves have not been let throughout the three years by reference to which the three last

[1] Rate of duty increased to 60 per cent by Finance Act, 1916, sec. 46 and to 80 per cent by Finance Act, 1917, sec. 21, *v. infra.*

prewar rent values are to be calculated, or for any other reason there are no proper data for ascertaining the prewar rent values, shall be taken to be such amount as may be fixed by the commissioners of inland revenue, having regard to the data afforded by the working and price of minerals in like circumstances, subject nevertheless to the same appeal as that to which the assessment of duty by the commissioners is subject under Part I of the Finance (1909–10) Act, 1910.

The prewar rent value shall, as respects each of the three years immediately preceding the first accounting year, be taken to be the sum to which the rent for the accounting year would amount if the rent, so far as variable according to price, were based on the average prices governing the payment of the rent in that year.

(3) Any amount payable in any accounting year by the lessee of minerals or wayleaves to a superior lessor as rent in respect of the minerals or wayleaves shall be treated as a deduction from the amount payable to the lessee as rent for that year, and in computing the prewar rent values a corresponding deduction shall be made on account of any such rent.

(4) Any increment value duty payable annually under section 22 of the Finance (1909–10) Act, 1910, shall, when paid, be treated as a deduction from the rent payable to any person in the year in which the duty is paid, and a corresponding deduction shall be made in computing the prewar standard with which the rent for that year is to be compared.

(5) Any duty payable under this section shall be assessed by the commissioners of inland revenue on the person liable, subject to the same appeal as that to which an assessment of duty by the commissioners under Part I of the Finance (1909–10) Act, 1910, is subject, and shall be recoverable as a debt due to His Majesty from that person.

(6) Subsection (3) of section 20 of the Finance (1909–10) Act, 1910, shall extend so as to authorize particulars to be required of any lease of minerals or wayleaves and as to the sums paid or payable thereunder, and of such other particulars as to the minerals or wayleaves as the commissioners may require for the purpose of this section.

(7) Expressions to which a special meaning is attached by Part I of the Finance (1909–10) Act, 1910, shall have the same meaning in this section.

RETURNS.

44. (1) The commissioners of inland revenue may, for the purposes of this part of this act, require any person engaged in any trade or business to which this part of this act applies, or who was so engaged during any accounting period or prewar trade year, to furnish them within two months after the requirement for the return is made with returns of the profits of the trade or business during the accounting period or prewar trade years and such other particulars in connection with the trade or business as the commissioners may require.

(2) It shall be the duty of every person chargeable to excess profits duty under this part of this act to give notice that he is chargeable to the commissioners of inland revenue before the 31st day of January, 1916, and it shall be the duty of the liquidator of every company

which is being wound up at the time of the commencement of this act or is wound up after the commencement of this act, and is chargeable to excess profits duty, to give notice of the fact to the commissioners of inland revenue.

If any person fails to furnish a proper return in accordance with this section or to comply with any requirement of the commissioners under this section, or to give any notice required by this section, he shall be liable on summary conviction to a fine not exceeding £100 and to a further fine not exceeding £10 a day for every day during which the offense continues after conviction therefor.

(3) A person shall not, for the purpose of avoiding the payment of excess-profits duty, enter into any fictitious or artificial transaction or carry out any fictitious or artificial operation, and, if he has entered into any such transaction or carried out any such operation before the commencement of this act, shall inform the commissioners of inland revenue of the nature of the transaction or operation.

If any person acts in contravention of or fails to comply with this provision, he shall be liable on summary conviction to a fine not exceeding £100.

SUPPLEMENTAL PROVISIONS.

45. (1) The excess-profits duty shall be assessed by the commissioners of inland revenue, and shall be payable at any time, not being less than two months, after it is assessed.

The commissioners may, in any case where they think fit, allow the duty to be paid in installments of such amount, payable at such times as the commissioners direct.

(2) The duty may be assessed on any person for the time being owning or carrying on the trade or business or acting as agent for that person in carrying on the trade or business, or, where a trade or business has ceased, on the person who owned or carried on the trade or business or acted as agent in carrying on the trade or business immediately before the time at which the trade or business ceased, and where there has been a change of ownership of the trade or business, the commissioners of inland revenue may, if they think fit, take the accounting period as the period ending on the date on which the ownership has so changed and assess the duty on the person who owned or carried on the trade or business or acted as agent for the person carrying on the trade or business at that date.

(3) The amount of duty payable shall be recoverable as a debt due to His Majesty from the person on whom it is assessed.

Any such amount shall, if it is less than £50, be recoverable also summarily as a civil debt.

(4) Where a company is wound up after the commencement of this act and before the 1st day of July, 1916, and the company would be chargeable with excess-profits duty if the provisions of this act were continued and extended to accounting periods ending before the 1st day of July, 1916, it shall be the duty of the liquidator of the company to give notice to the commissioners of inland revenue, and to set aside such sum out of the assets of the company as appears to the commissioners of inland revenue to be sufficient to provide for any such excess-profits duty as may become chargeable.

(5) Any person who is dissatisfied with the amount of any assessment made upon him by the commissioners of inland revenue under

this part of this act may (except in cases where a special right of appeal is given under this part of this act) appeal to the general commissioners for the division in which he is assessed, or to the special commissioners, and those commissioners shall have power on any appeal, if they think fit, to summon witnesses and examine them upon oath.

The power under sections 21 and 22 of the Income-Tax Act, 1853, to require an appeal in Ireland to the special commissioners to be reheard by the county court judge, or chairman of quarter sessions, or recorder shall apply to an appeal in Ireland under this provision.

Section 59 of the Taxes Management Act, 1880 (which relates to the statement of a case on a point of law), shall apply with the necessary modifications in the case of any appeal to the general or special commissioners under this section, or of the rehearing of any such appeal in Ireland, and in the case of a reference to the board of referees under this part of this act, as it applies in the case of appeals to the general or special commissioners under the income-tax acts.

(6) The duty assessed by the commissioners of inland revenue shall be payable notwithstanding any appeal under this section, except in cases where the commissioners of inland revenue direct to the contrary, but the commissioners shall make such repayments, if any, as are necessary to give effect to any decision on appeal as soon as possible after such decision has been given.

(7) The commissioners of inland revenue may make regulations with respect to the assessment and collection of the excess-profits duty and the hearing of appeals under this section, and may by those regulations apply and adapt any enactments relating to the assessment and collection of income tax, or the hearing of appeals as to income tax by the general or special commissioners, which do not otherwise apply.

(8) All commissioners and other persons employed for any purpose in connection with the assessment or collection of excess-profits duty shall be subject to the same obligations as to secrecy with respect to excess-profits duty as those persons are subject to with respect to income tax, and any oath taken by any such person as to secrecy with respect to income tax shall be deemed to extend also to secrecy with respect to excess-profits duty.

FOURTH SCHEDULE.

PART I. COMPUTATION OF PROFITS.

1. The profits shall be taken to be the actual profits arising in the accounting period, and the principle of computing profits by reference to any other year or an average of years shall not be followed.

2. The principle of the income-tax acts under which deductions are not allowed for interest on money borrowed for the purpose of the trade or business, or for rent, or royalties, or for other payments income tax on which is collected at the source (not being payments of dividends or payments for the distribution of profits), and under which profits or gains arising from lands, tenements, or hereditaments forming part of the assets of the trade or business are excluded shall not be followed.

3. Deductions for wear and tear or for any expenditure of a capital nature for renewals, or for the development of the trade or business or otherwise in respect of the trade or business, shall not be allowed except such as may be allowed under the income-tax acts, and if allowed shall be only of such amount as appears to the commissioners of inland revenue to be reasonably and properly attributable to the year or accounting period.

4. Deductions shall not be allowed on account of the liability to pay or the payment of income tax or excess-profits duty, but a deduction shall be allowed (if not otherwise allowed by means of the adoption of the principle of the income-tax acts) for any sum which has been paid in respect of the profits on account of any excess-profits duty or similar duty imposed in any country outside the United Kingdom.[1]

5. Any deduction allowed for the remuneration of directors, managers, and persons concerned in the management of the trade or business shall not, unless the commissioners of inland revenue, owing to any special circumstances or to the fact that the remuneration of any managers or managing directors depends on the profits of the trade or business, otherwise direct, exceed the sums allowed for those purposes in the last prewar trade year or a proportionate part thereof, as the case requires, and no deduction shall be allowed in respect of any transaction or operation of any nature, where it appears, or to the extent to which it appears, that the transaction or operation has artificially reduced the amount to be taken as the amount of the profits of the trade or business for the purposes of this act.

6. Where any company, either in its own name or that of a nominee, owns the whole of the ordinary capital of any other company carrying on the same trade or business or so much of that capital as under the general law a single shareholder can legally own, the provisions of Part III of this act as to excess-profits duty and the prewar standard of profits shall apply as if that other company were a branch of the first-named company, and the profits of the two companies shall not be separately assessed.

7. Where in the case of any trade or business—

(*a*) The percentage standard is adopted as the prewar standard of profits; and

(*b*) The net result of the trade or business during the three last prewar trade years has shown a loss; and

(*c*) Any part of the profits has been applied in extinction of that loss—

then in estimating the profits a deduction shall be allowed equal to the amount of profits so applied.

8. In estimating the profits no account shall be taken of income received from investments except in the case of life assurance businesses and businesses where the principal business consists of the making of investments. Where account is taken of any such income—

(*a*) Any variation in the value of any of those investments which appears to the commissioners of inland revenue not to be due to a variation in profits shall also be taken into account; and

[1] Cf. provisions for relief in respect of Colonial excess-profits duty in Finance Act, 1917, sec. 23, *infra*.

(*b*) Where the income has been derived from profits in respect of which any payment or repayment of excess-profits duty has been made under this act, such deduction or addition shall be made in computing the profits as will make proper allowance for that payment or repayment of duty.

9. In computing the total profits of a local authority from any trades or businesses carried on by that authority the total amount which is required to be raised by them out of the rates or otherwise, for sinking-fund purposes in connection with those trades or businesses shall be allowed as a deduction.

10. In the case of societies registered under the industrial and provident societies acts the excess-profits duty shall be charged on the sum by which the profits per member for the accounting period (including any surplus arising from transactions with members) exceed the like profits per member in the prewar trade year or average of years taken as the basis of computation for the purpose of the prewar standard of profits, multiplied by the number of members in the accounting period.[1]

11. In the case of any contract extending beyond one accounting period from the date of its commencement to the completion thereof and only partially performed in any accounting period there shall (unless the commissioners of inland revenue, owing to any special circumstances, otherwise direct) be attributed to each of the accounting periods in which such contract was partially performed, such proportion of the entire profits or loss or estimated profits or loss in respect of the complete performance of the contract as shall be properly attributable to such accounting periods, respectively, having regard to the extent to which the contract was performed in such periods.

Part II. Prewar Standard.

1. The profits of any prewar trade year shall be computed on the same principles and subject to the same provisions as the profits of the accounting period are computed.

2. Where the accounting period for which the excess profits duty is to be assessed is less than a year, the amount of the prewar standard of profit shall be proportionately reduced.

3. Where it is shown to the satisfaction of the commissioners of inland revenue in the case of any trade or business that the three last prewar trade years have been years of abnormal depression, any four of the last six prewar trade years may be substituted for the purposes of the prewar standard of profits for any two of the three last prewar trade years.

The three last prewar trade years shall not be considered as years of abnormal depression unless the average profits of those years have been at least 25 per cent lower than the average profits of the preceding three years.

4. Where, owing to the recent commencement of a trade or business there have not been three prewar trade years, but there have been two prewar trade years, the prewar standard of profits shall be taken to be the amount of the profits arising from the trade or business (on the average of those two years or, at the option of the tax-

[1] An alternative method of computing the excess-profits duty in this case is provided in the Finance Act, 1917, sec. 26 (8) *v. infra.*

payer, the profits arising from the trade or business) during the last of those two years, and where there have not been two prewar trade years, but there has been one prewar trade year, the prewar standard of profits shall be taken to be the profits arising from the trade or business during that year, and where there has not been one prewar trade year, the prewar standard of profits shall be taken to be the statutory percentage[1] on the average amount of capital employed in the trade or business during the accounting period.

Where the trade or business is an agency or business of a nature involving capital of a comparatively small amount, the prewar standard of profits shall be computed by reference to the profits arising from any trade, business, office, employment, or profession of any sort, whether liable to excess-profits duty or not, carried on by the agent or other person before his new trade or business commenced as if it was the same trade or business; but only to the extent to which the income from the former trade, business, office, employment, or profession has been diminished.

5. Where since the commencement of the three last prewar trade years a trade or business has changed ownership, the provisions of this part of this schedule shall apply as if a new trade or business had been commenced on the change of ownership, except in cases when the taxpayer makes an application that the provisions of Part III of this act and this schedule should apply as if the trade or business had not changed ownership, but in that case such modifications (if any) shall be made in the application of this schedule as may be necessary to make the basis on which the profits standard is computed the same as that on which the profits of the accounting period are computed.

6. It is hereby declared that where any business or trade is confined to the management of any particular assets, but power exists to substitute other assets for those particular assets, or any of them, such a substitution shall not be deemed, for the purposes of Part III of this act, to constitute a change of ownership of the business; but where any such substitution has been carried out by the sale of assets and the purchase of other assets the capital of the trade or business shall be taken to be increased or decreased, as the case may be, only by the amount of the difference between the price of the assets purchased and the price obtained for the assets sold, and the capital representing the assets purchased shall be estimated on the same basis for all the purposes of Part III of this act.

PART III. CAPITAL.

1. The amount of the capital of a trade or business shall, so far as it does not consist of money, be taken to be—

(*a*) So far as it consists of assets acquired by purchase, the price at which those assets were acquired, subject to any proper deductions for wear and tear or replacement, or for unpaid purchase money; and

(*b*) So far as it consists of assets being debts due to the trade or business, the nominal amount of those debts, subject to any reduction which has been allowed in respect of those debts for income-tax purposes; and

[1] Three per cent added to this by Finance Act, 1917, sec. 26 (1).

(*c*) So far as it consists of any other assets which have not been acquired by purchase, the value of the assets at the time when they became assets of the trade or business, subject to any proper deductions for wear and tear or replacement.

Nothing in this part of this schedule shall prevent accumulated profits employed in the business being treated as capital.

2. Any capital the income on which is not taken into account for the purposes of Part I of this schedule, and any borrowed money or debts, shall be deducted in computing the amount of capital for the purposes of Part III of this act.

3. Where any asset has been paid for otherwise than in cash the cost price of that asset shall be taken to be the value of the consideration at the time the asset was acquired, but where a trade or business has been converted into a company and the shares in the company are wholly or mainly held by the person who was owner of the trade or business no value shall be attached to those shares so far as they are represented by good will or otherwise than by material assets of the company unless the commissioners of inland revenue in special circumstances otherwise direct. Patents and secret processes shall be deemed to be material assets.

Finance Act, 1916.

[6 and 7 Geo. V, c. 24.]

PART III.

EXCESS-PROFITS DUTY.

CONTINUANCE AND INCREASE OF RATE.

45. (1) The Finance (No. 2) Act, 1915 (in this part of this act referred to as the principal act), shall, so far as it relates to excess-profits duty, apply, unless Parliament otherwise determines, to any accounting period ending on or after the 1st day of July, 1915, and before the 1st day of August, 1917, as it applies to accounting periods ended after the 4th day of August, 1914, and before the said 1st day of July.

(2) Section 38 of the principal act shall, as respects excess profits arising in any accounting period beginning after the expiration of a year from the commencement of the first accounting period, have effect as if 60 per cent[1] of the excess were substituted as the rate of duty for 50 per cent of the excess.

---

[1] Rate of duty increased to 80 per cent by Finance Act, 1917, sec. 20, *v infra*.

Where part of an accounting period is after and part before the date of the expiration of a year from the commencement of the first accounting period, the total excess profits and any deficiencies or losses arising in the accounting period shall be apportioned between the time up to and including, and the time after, that date in proportion to the length of those times, respectively, and the rate attributable to the time after and the time before and including that date shall, respectively, be 60 and 50 per cent of the excess.

In the case of trades or businesses commencing after the 4th day of August, 1914, the rate of duty shall be 60 per cent of the excess in respect of any accounting period ending after the 4th day of August, 1915.

In calculating any repayment or set off under subsection (3) of section 38 of the principal act any amount to be repaid or set off on account of a deficiency or loss arising in any period in respect of which duty would be payable at the rate of 50 per cent of the excess, shall be calculated by reference to that rate of duty.

Any additional duty payable by virtue of this section in respect of a past accounting period may be assessed and recovered notwithstanding that duty has already been assessed in respect of that period.

(3) It shall be the duty of every person chargeable to excess-profits duty under Part III of the principal act, as extended by this act, if he has not previously given notice of his liability to be charged with excess-profits duty in respect of any accounting period, to give notice to the commissioners of inland revenue before the expiration of two months after the termination of any accounting period in respect of which he is chargeable, or, if the accounting period terminated before the passing of this act, within one month after the passing of this act.

If any person fails to give the notice required by this provision he shall be liable on summary conviction to a fine not exceeding £100, and to a further fine not exceeding £10 a day for every day during which the offense continues after conviction therefor.

INCREASE OF RATE OF EXCESS MINERAL RIGHTS DUTY.

46. (1) Section 43 of the principal act (which relates to excess mineral rights duty) shall have effect as if 60 per cent[1] of the excess were substituted as the rate of duty for 50 per cent of the excess, in the case of minerals which have become subject to a mining lease after the 4th day of August, 1914, for all accounting years, and in the case of other minerals for any accounting year ending after the completion of the first accounting year, and any additional duty may be recovered accordingly.

(2) It is hereby declared that the words in subsection (1) of section 43 of the principal act "assets of any trade or business" refer only to assets of the trade or business of the person receiving the rent for the right to work the minerals or for the mineral way leaves.

[1] Rate of duty increased to 80 per cent by Finance Act, 1917, sec. 21, *v. infra*.

COMPUTATION IN CASE OF SALE OF SHIPS.

47. Where any ship has been sold since the 4th day of August, 1914, in such circumstances that the profits of the sale are not the profits of a trade or business, the following special provisions shall, if the commissioners of inland revenue so require, be applied in the computation of the liability to excess-profits duty in respect of the profits arising from the use of the ship:

(*a*) The prewar standard of profits of the purchaser as respects the ship shall, where the standard of the trade or business of the vendor is a profits standard, be calculated by reference to the profits arising from the use of the ship during the prewar trade years, and shall be ascertained in accordance with the provisions of the principal act, but calculated, where necessary, as if the use of the ship were a separate business: and where that standard is a percentage standard the prewar standard of profits as respects the ship shall be the same as if the ship had not been sold, or, in the case of a ship which was used for the first time after the 4th day of August, 1914, shall be calculated by reference to the capital represented by the ship at the date when it was first used: and the prewar standard of profits of the trade or business of the vendor and of the purchaser shall respectively be reduced and increased as the case may require, with any adjustments which may be necessary to meet the case of borrowed money or unpaid purchase money or other similar matters.

(*b*) For the purpose of estimating separately the profits arising from the use of the ship, an apportionment shall, where necessary, be made of the total profits of the trade or business in which the ship has been used, regard being had to the earnings of the ship as compared with the earnings of the other assets employed in the trade or business.

Any appeal under subsection (5) of section 45 of the principal act, so far as it involves any question of an apportionment under this provision, shall be to the special commissioners.

(*c*) The power to require returns under subsection (1) of section 44 of the principal act shall include power for the commissioners of inland revenue to require any vendor of the ship to give such information to them and to the purchaser as the commissioners think necessary in order to enable the provisions of this section to be carried into effect.

(*d*) Nothing in subsection (3) of section 40 of the principal act or in paragraph 3 of Part I of the Fourth Schedule to the principal act shall operate so as to enable the purchaser of the ship to obtain any greater relief than could have been obtained by the vendor if the ship had not been sold, other than relief in connection with expenditure by the purchaser on improvements or repairs.

(*e*) In the application of section 41 of the principal act to any trade or business whose prewar standard of profits has been determined or adjusted under this section any increase or decrease of capital attributable to the purchase or sale of the ship shall be disregarded, and where any such determination or adjustment has taken place both in respect of the sale of a ship and the purchase of another ship, for the same trade or business, paragraph 6 of Part II of the Fourth Schedule to the principal act shall not apply.

ADJUSTMENT IN CASE OF CONTROLLED ESTABLISHMENTS.

48. (1) The commissioners of inland revenue may treat any sums actually paid in respect of munitions exchequer payments,[1] which appear to the commissioners to be attributable to the same period and subject matter as that for which excess-profits duty is to be paid, as a payment on account of excess-profits duty, or, if the amount of the munitions exchequer payments is larger than the amount payable as excess-profits duty, as extinguishing the duty for the purposes of collection; and may arrange with the minister of munitions, if in any case excess-profits duty is paid before the munitions exchequer payment, for the deduction of excess-profits duty payments from any sums to be collected in respect of munitions exchequer payments which appear to the commissioners to be attributable to the same period and subject matter as that for which the excess-profits duty payments have been made, or, if the amount of the excess-profits duty payments is greater than the amount to be collected on account of munitions exchequer payments, for the extinction of the amount to be so collected.

For the purpose of determining the period to which any profits are to be attributed under this section, profits shall be deemed to accrue from day to day at a uniform rate.

(2) Any excess-profits duty and any munitions exchequer payments which are remitted under this section for the purpose of collection shall not be deemed to have been paid for the purposes of section 35 of the principal act (which relates to computation of profits and gains in relation to excess-profits duty) as extended by this act.

(3) Deductions shall not be allowed on account of munitions exchequer payments in computing profits for the purpose of excess-profits duty.

DIRECTORS' FEES.

49. (1) Where the prewar standard of profits is taken to be the percentage standard or is calculated by reference to the statutory percentage in the case of any trade or business owned or carried on by a company or other body corporate whose directors have a controlling interest, the commissioners of inland revenue may, if they think fit, as respects any accounting period, including a past accounting period, for the purpose of the provisions relating to the statutory percentage and for the purpose of the determination and computation of profits under Part I of the Fourth Schedule to the principal act, treat the company or body corporate as if it were a firm and not a company or body corporate and the directors or any of them as if they were partners in the firm.

(2) If as respects any accounting period ending on or after the first day of July, 1915, the commissioners of inland revenue refuse to allow a deduction in respect of any increase in the remuneration of directors of any trade or business, and the taxpayer is required to pay excess-profits duty in respect of the disallowed deduction, the taxpayer shall be entitled to recover from any such director the amount which the taxpayer has paid by way of excess-profits duty in respect of the increase; but any amount so recovered shall, unless the commissioners otherwise direct, be treated as excess-profits duty paid

[1] Defined in sec. 57, *infra*. These payments cease as regards any profits arising after Dec. 31, 1916, by sec. 24 of the Finance Act, 1917 (*q. v.*).

by the director from whom it is recovered and not as excess-profits duty paid by the taxpayer.

(3) In this section the expression "directors" includes any managers or persons concerned in the management of the trade or business who are remunerated out of the funds of the trade or business.

PROFITS APPLIED IN EXTINCTION OF PREVIOUS LOSSES.

50. Paragraph 7 of Part I of the Fourth Schedule of the principal act (which allows deductions to be made in respect of profits applied in extinction of losses) shall apply to a case where the capital account of any trade or business shows a debit balance as it applies to a case where the percentage standard is adopted as the prewar standard of profits.

ACCOUNTING PERIOD.

51. It is hereby declared that, for the purpose of subsection (2) of section 38 of the principal act, any period for which the books of a trade or business have been actually made up for any interim or other purpose in such a manner that the profits for that period can be readily ascertained is (without prejudice to the powers of the commissioners of inland revenue under that provision) to be taken as an accounting period, notwithstanding that under the articles of association of the company carrying on the trade or business or under any other regulations affecting the carrying on of the trade or business the accounts are also required to be made up for some other period, and notwithstanding that such accounts are not issued.

ACCUMULATING PROFITS.

52. It is hereby declared that, for the purpose of excess-profits duty, profits of any trade or business arising and accumulating during any accounting period are not, during that period, to be treated as accumulated profits within the meaning of Part III of the Fourth Schedule to the principal act, or as capital employed in the trade or business.

MUNITIONS EXCHEQUER PAYMENTS.

53. Section 35 of the principal act (which relates to the computation of profits and gains for the purpose of income tax in relation to excess-profits duty) shall apply to sums actually paid in respect of munitions exchequer payments as it applies to excess-profits duty, except that the relief to the taxpayer under subsection (2) of that section shall in all cases be given by means of repayment and not by deduction.

DEPOSIT OF SUMS FOR PAYMENT.

54. Any person may deposit with the commissioners of inland revenue any sums for the purpose of satisfying any excess-profits duty which may thereafter become payable by him; and sums so deposited shall be applied in payment of any such duty as and when it becomes payable.

In calculating the amount to be so applied in payment of duty interest shall be allowed at such rate as may for the time being be determined by the Treasury.

CONTROLLED ESTABLISHMENTS—BOARD OF REFEREES.

55. Subsection (3) of section 40 of the principal act (which provides, amongst other things, for the reference of certain matters for the decision of a board of referees) shall, where the application for such a reference is made in respect of a trade or business carried on in a controlled establishment within the meaning of Part II of the Munitions of War Act, 1915, and relates to an accounting period during any part of which the establishment has been so controlled, and to the postponement or suspension of renewals or repairs, or to exceptional depreciation or obsolescence of assets, or to the necessity in connection with the present war of providing plant, have effect as though a referee or board of referees appointed or designated by the minister of munitions for the purpose were substituted for the board of referees under the principal act.

EXEMPTION OF BUSINESSES CARRIED ON UNDER THE COURT.

56. In the case of any trade or business which by reason of its being unable to pay its debenture holders or creditors is being carried on by a liquidator, receiver, or trustee under the court, no excess-profits duty shall be levied or paid until provision has been made for payment of such unpaid debenture holders or creditors.

DEFINITION OF MUNITIONS EXCHEQUER PAYMENTS.

57. In this part of this act the expression "munitions exchequer payments" means any sums paid into the exchequer under section 4 of the Munitions of War Act, 1915, on account of the excess of the net profits of a controlled establishment.

Finance Act, 1917.

[7 and 8 Geo V, c. 31.]

PART III

EXCESS-PROFITS DUTY.

CONTINUANCE AND INCREASE.

20. (1) The Finance (No. 2) Act, 1915 (in this part of this act referred to as the principal act), shall, so far as it relates to excess-profits duty, apply, unless Parliament otherwise determines, to any accounting period ending on or after the 1st day of August, 1917, and before the 1st day of August, 1918, as it applies to accounting periods

ended after the 4th day of August, 1914, and before the 1st day of August, 1917.

(2) Section 38 of the principal act shall, as respects excess profits arising in any accounting period commencing on or after the 1st day of January, 1917, have effect as if 80 per cent of the excess were substituted as the rate of duty for 60 per cent of the excess, or, in the case of an accounting period which commenced before that date but ends after that date, as if 80 per cent were substituted for 60 per cent as respects so much of the excess as may be apportioned under this act to the part commencing on that date.

In calculating any repayment or set-off under subsection (3) of section 38 of the principal act any amount to be repaid or set-off on account of a deficiency or loss arising in any accounting period commencing on or after the 1st day of January, 1917, or, in the case of an accounting period which has commenced before that date but ends after that date, on account of so much of the deficiency or loss as may be apportioned under this act to the part commencing on that date, shall be calculated by reference to duty at the rate of 80 per cent.

Any additional duty payable by virtue of this section in respect of a past accounting period may be assessed and recovered notwithstanding that duty has already been assessed in respect of that period.

(3) It shall be the duty of every person chargeable to excess-profits duty, if he has not previously given notice of his liability to be charged with excess-profits duty in respect of any accounting period, to give notice to the commissioners within two months after the termination of any accounting period in respect of which he is chargeable, or, if the accounting period terminated before the passing of this act, within one month after the passing of this act.

If any person fails to give the notice required by this provision he shall be liable on summary conviction to a fine not exceeding £100, and to a further fine not exceeding £10 a day for every day during which the offense continues after conviction therefor.

INCREASE OF RATE OF EXCESS MINERAL RIGHTS DUTY.

21. Section 43 of the principal act (which relates to excess mineral rights duty) shall have effect as if 80 per cent of the excess were substituted as the rate of duty for 60 per cent for any accounting year commencing on or after the 1st day of January, 1917, or, in the case of an accounting year which commenced before that date but ends after that date, as if 80 per cent were substituted for 60 per cent as respects so much of the excess as may be apportioned under this act to the part commencing on that date, and any additional duty may be recovered accordingly:

Provided, That where it is shown to the satisfaction of the commissioners that the amount payable as rent under any lease or agreement for a lease for any accounting year in respect of which or any part of which excess mineral rights duty is payable at the rate of 80 per cent is not greater than the average amount payable as rent for the two prewar years the prices in which are selected by the taxpayer for the purpose of determining the prewar rent values of the rent for the accounting year, or would be reduced below that amount by the payment of excess mineral rights duty, no excess mineral rights duty or, as the case may be, such an amount of excess mineral rights duty only as will reduce the amount payable as rent for the accounting year to the said average amount, shall be paid for that accounting year.

DEFICIENCIES AND LOSSES OF SHIPPING CONCERNS.

22. (1) In computing the excess-profits duty of any trade or business which consists wholly or partly of the business of shipping, the provisions of subsection (3) of section 38 of the principal act (which relate to the repayment or setting off of duty on account of deficiencies or losses) shall not apply in relation to any deficiency or loss in any accounting period commencing on or after the 1st day of January, 1917, and in the case of an accounting period which has commenced before that date but ends after that date, shall not apply in relation to so much of the deficiency or loss as may be apportioned under this act to the part commencing on that date:

Provided, That—

(*a*) Where the shipping business is carried on merely as ancillary to the principal trade or business, the provisions of this section shall not apply:

(*b*) Where the trade or business carried on does not consist wholly of shipping, and the part which does not consist of shipping is not merely ancillary to the business of shipping, such apportionment of any deficiency or loss shall be made by the commissioners as may be necessary to limit the application of this section to such part of the business as consists of shipping: and

(*c*) If in any such accounting period as aforesaid there has been a loss or the profits have not reached the point which would have involved liability to excess-profits duty if the percentage standard had been adopted, the same amount shall, as respects the deficiency or loss or so much thereof as is affected by this section, be repaid or set off under subsection (3) of the said section 38 as would have been repaid or set off if the percentage standard had been adopted.

(2) Any appeal under subsection (5) of section 45 of the principal act on any question arising under this section shall be to the special commissioners.

(3) In this section the expression "business of shipping" means the business carried on by an owner of ships, and for the purposes of this definition the expression "owner" includes any charterer to whom a ship is demised.

RELIEF IN RESPECT OF COLONIAL EXCESS-PROFITS DUTY.

23. (1) His Majesty may by order in council declare—

(*a*) That under the law in force in any of His Majesty's possessions excess-profits duty is chargeable in respect of any profits in respect of which excess-profits duty is also payable in the United Kingdom; and

(*b*) That arrangements have been made with the Government of any such possession whereby, in respect of any profits, only the duty which is higher in amount is to be payable, and the amount of such duty is to be apportioned between the respective exchequers in proportion to the amount of duty which would otherwise have been payable in the United Kingdom and in that possession, respectively.

(2) Where any such order in council is made, then, if the commissioners are satisfied that any case is one to which any such arrangements relate, they may, in lieu of any relief granted under paragraph 4 of Part I of the Fourth Schedule to the principal act, allow or make such remission or adjustments of duty as may be necessary to give effect to such arrangements, so, however, that the effect of such remission or adjustments shall not be less favorable than the relief in lieu of which they are allowed or made.

(3) The obligation as to secrecy imposed by subsection (8) of section 45 of the principal act shall not prevent the disclosure to the Government of the possession concerned of such facts as may be necessary to enable such arrangements as aforesaid to be carried into effect.

MUNITIONS EXCHEQUER PAYMENTS.

24. (1) The provisions of section 4 of the Munitions of War Act, 1915, with respect to munitions exchequer payments shall not apply to any profits arising after the 31st day of December, 1916, or apportioned under this act to the period after that date.

(2) Munitions exchequer payments arising on or before the 31st day of December, 1916, or apportioned under this act to the period down to and including that date shall, after the passing of this act, be assessed and collected, or, if already assessed but not collected, collected by the commissioners, and shall be computed by them in accordance with the provisions of that act and the rules made thereunder, and the commissioners shall for those purposes have all the powers of the minister of munitions, including the power of making rules.

For the purposes of such assessment and collection, the provisions for the time being in force with respect to the assessment and collection of excess-profits duty (including provisions as to returns and penalties, but excluding provisions imposing any charge of duty or as to the computation of duty) shall apply, and rules may be made by the commissioners accordingly, and the provisions of section 48 of the Finance Act, 1916, relating to the adjustment of excess-profits duty and munitions exchequer payments, shall apply subject to such modifications as may be necessary in consequence of the transfer of powers effected by this subsection.

Any rules made by the commissioners may specify matters which may be referred to the minister, or to a referee or board of referees appointed by him, and prescribe the manner in which such cases are to be referred.

(3) For the purposes of subsection (3) of section 5 of the said act, any establishments in which the same person has a controlling or preponderating interest may, if the commissioners so determine, be treated as belonging to the same owner.

(4) Subsections (2) and (3) of section 49 of the Finance Act, 1916 (which relate to the recovery of payments in respect of increased directors' fees), shall apply for the purposes of munitions exchequer payments as they apply for the purposes of excess-profits duty, with the necessary modifications.

REFERENCE TO REFEREES.

25. Notwithstanding anything contained in section 42 of the principal act (which provides for the reference to the board of referees of questions as to percentages, etc.), the commissioners may, if they think fit, refer to the board of referees any application made under that section as respects a class of trade or business, although the application may relate to matters already decided by that board, and the board may, if they think fit, on cause being shown by additional evidence or otherwise, reopen the case and make any order which they could have made on an application relating to matters not already decided by them, and may revise any order previously made by them affecting that class of trade or business; and any such order or revised order shall, as from such date as may be specified therein, apply and have effect in lieu of any previous order relating to the same matter

AMENDMENTS RELATING TO DEDUCTIONS, ETC.

26. In the application of Part III of the principal act to excess-profits duty for any accounting period ending after the 31st day of December, 1916, the following provisions shall have effect:

(1) In ascertaining the deduction to be made from the profits of the accounting period in respect of increased capital, or the prewar standard of profits in cases where there has not been one prewar trade year, 3 per cent shall be added to the statutory percentage per annum; and accordingly in subsection (1) of section 41 of, and paragraph 4 of Part II of the Fourth Schedule to, the principal act, the expression "statutory percentage" shall be taken to mean the statutory percentage as so increased.

(2) The statutory percentage shall, in the case of a trade or business not carried on or owned by a company or other body corporate, be taken to be 8 per cent instead of 7 per cent; and accordingly subsection (2) of section 40 of the principal act shall have effect as though 8 per cent were substituted for 7 per cent.

Provided, That nothing in this provision shall affect the amount of the statutory percentage for the purposes of subsection (2) of section 41 of the principal act.

(3) Any increase of the statutory percentage under this section shall be in addition to any increase of the statutory percentage which has, before the passing of this act, been made under section 42 of the principal act.

(4) Where the prewar standard of profits of any trade or business does not exceed £500 and the profits of the accounting period after any adjustment in respect of increased or decreased capital are less than £2,000, subsection (1) of section 38 of the principal act shall have effect as though for £200 there were substituted £200 with the addition of one-fifth of the amount by which the profits of the accounting period are less than £2,000, so, however, that if there has been a loss in the accounting period, then for the purpose of ascertaining the amount of any repayment or set-off under the principal act the addition allowed shall be such as if there had been neither loss nor profit; and that where the accounting period is a period of less than a year this provision shall have effect as if there were substituted for £2,000 and £200, respectively, a proportionately reduced amount.

The foregoing provision shall apply where the prewar standard of profits exceeds £500, subject to this qualification, that the amount of the addition shall be reduced by the amount by which the prewar standard exceeds £500.

(5) Where the commissioners are satisfied—

(*a*) That in connection with any trade or business two or more distinct and independent industries are carried on in separate establishments, and with books kept in such a manner that the profits in respect to each industry can be readily ascertained; and

(*b*) That in any year by reference to which the prewar standard of profits is calculated a loss has been sustained in respect of any one or more of such industries—

the commissioners may, if they think fit, in computing the profits standard, disregard that loss:

(6) Where the commissioners are satisfied that during the last six prewar trade years, owing to trading losses—

(*a*) Any former assets of any trade or business have ceased to form part of the assets of that trade or business; or

(*b*) The money borrowed in respect of the trade or business or the debts of the trade or business have increased; the commissioner shall, for the purpose of ascertaining the capital of the trade or business in any case where the percentage standard is adopted, compute the capital as though there had been no such loss of assets or increase of borrowed money or debts:

(7) Six years shall be substituted for three years in subsection (4) of section 41 of the principal act (which provides for the adjustment of excess-profits duty in respect of unremunerative capital).

(8) The excess-profits duty of a society registered under the industrial and provident societies acts may, if the society so requires, instead of being computed as provided for by paragraph 10 of Part I of the Fourth Schedule to the principal act, be computed as follows:

The amount of excess profits (if any) arising on commercial transactions with nonmembers shall be separately ascertained in accordance with the general principles of the principal act, and there shall be added thereto the amount (if any) by which the profit or surplus arising from transactions with members per pound sterling of turnover in the accounting period exceeds the like profit or surplus in the prewar trade year or average of years taken as the basis of computation for the purpose of the prewar standard of profits in respect of such commercial transactions as aforesaid, multiplied by the number of pounds sterling of turnover in the accounting period; and excess-profits duty shall be charged on the sum of those amounts:

Provided, That the method of computation hereby laid down shall not be adopted for ascertaining the amount of any deficiency or loss for the purposes of subsection (3) of section 38 of the principal act, nor shall any duty computed under this provision be repaid or remitted by reason of a deficiency or loss in any other accounting period computed as provided for by the said paragraph 10.

Regulations made by the commissioners for the purpose of carrying the foregoing provision into effect may provide for defining and ascertaining turnover and the profit or surplus per pound sterling thereof, and for the application of that provision to new societies, and for extending, subject to such modifications as may be prescribed, to cases where duty is computed under that provision any of the general principles of the principal act as to relief from duty.

APPORTIONMENT OF ACCOUNTING PERIODS AND YEARS.

27. Where part of an accounting period or of an accounting year, or of any period in respect of part of which munitions exchequer payments are chargeable, is after, and part before, the beginning of the 1st day of January, 1917, the total excess profits and any deficiencies or losses arising in any such accounting period, and the total excess rent for any such accounting year, and the total profits in respect of part of which munitions exchequer payments are chargeable, shall be apportioned between the time up to and the time after that date in proportion to the number of months or fractions of months before and after that date, respectively.

INTERPRETATION.

28. In this part of this act references to the principal act or to the Munitions of War Act, 1915, or to any provisions of those acts, shall be construed as references to those acts or provisions as amended by any subsequent enactment, and the expression "the commissioners" means the commissioners of inland revenue, and the expression "munitions exchequer payments" in this part of this act and in any other enactment includes any sums payable into the exchequer under section 4 of the munitions of war act, 1915, on account of the excess of the net profits of a controlled establishment.

FINANCE BILL, 1918.

[Introduced in the House of Commons, May 1; Part III adopted without amendment in committee of the whole, June 4.]

PART III

EXCESS-PROFITS DUTY.

CONTINUATION.

34. The Finance (No. 2) Act, 1915 (in this part of this act referred to as "the principal act"), as amended or extended by any subsequent enactment, shall, so far as it relates to excess-profits duty, apply, unless Parliament otherwise determines, to any accounting period ending on or after the 1st day of August, 1918, and before the 1st day of August, 1919, as it applies to accounting periods ended after the 4th day of August, 1914, and before the 1st day of August, 1918.

PROFITS ARISING FROM SALE OF TRADING STOCK.

35. (1) For the purposes of excess-profits duty the profits arising from the sale at any time after the 22d day of April, 1918, otherwise than in the ordinary course of trade of the trading stock or part of the trading stock belonging or formerly belonging to any trade or business shall be deemed to be profits arising from a trade or business, and where any such sale takes place after a trade or business has ceased the trade or business shall be deemed to have been carried on up to and including the date on which the sale takes place, and

the accounting period shall be taken to be such as the commissioners of inland revenue may determine.

(2) Where a trade or business has ceased but is deemed for the purposes of this section to have been carried on for any period—

(*a*) The person by whom or by whose authority any trading stock is sold, whether as owner, agent, liquidator, trustee, or receiver, or other person acting in a similar capacity, shall be deemed to be the person carrying on the trade or business, and excess-profits duty shall be assessed on and recoverable from that person, and nothing in subsection (2) of section 45 of the principal act shall operate so as to impose any liability to duty on the purchaser of the trading stock; and

(*b*) The appointment of any such liquidator, trustee, or receiver, or other person shall not be treated as a change of ownership of the trade or business, and subsection (3) of section 38 of the principal act and paragraph 7 of Part I of the Fourth Schedule to that act as amended by any subsequent enactment shall have effect as if the profits arising from the sale of the trading stock had been made by the owner of the business immediately before the appointment of the liquidator, trustee, receiver, or other person and as if the duty were payable by him.

(3) Where any trading stock is sold together with other assets of the trade or business, the part of the consideration attributable to the trading stock shall, subject to appeal in manner provided by subsection (5) of section 45 of the principal act, be determined by the commissioners of inland revenue, and the part of the consideration so determined shall be deemed to be the price paid for the trading stock by the purchaser.

(4) For the purpose of this section any trading stock which has been disposed of otherwise than by way of sale shall be deemed to have been sold, and any such trading stock so disposed of, and any trading stock which has been sold for a consideration other than cash, not being a consideration the value of which can be easily ascertained, shall be deemed to have realized the market price of the day on which it was so disposed of or sold.

No person shall at any time after the 14th day of May, 1918, dispose otherwise than by way of sale of any trading stock unless he has previously made provision to the satisfaction of the commissioners of inland revenue for securing the payment of any excess-profits duty which may be chargeable by virtue of the provisions of this section, and if any person attemps to dispose of any trading stock in contravention of this provision the disposal shall be void and of no effect.

(5) In this section the expression "trading stock" includes—

(*a*) Any goods such as are sold in the ordinary course of a trade or business whether in a finished condition or not; and

(*b*) Any raw or other materials used in the manufacture or preparation of any such goods, and references to disposal of trading stock do not include disposal by way of testamentary disposition.

Regulations Prescribed by the Commissioners of Inland Revenue, Dated January 6. 1916.

(Statutory Rules and Orders, 1916, No. 1, pp 348-350.)

1. Subject to the express provisions of the act and these regulations, the sections of the Income Tax Acts enumerated in the schedule to these regulations shall, with the modifications therein described, apply to the assessment and collection of excess profits duty and the hearing of appeals in connection therewith

2. If in any case any person required by law to make a return fails to do so, or if the return made by him appears to the commissioners of inland revenue to be incorrect or insufficient, the commissioners may, without prejudice to the enforcement of any penalty which may have been incurred, make an assessment of excess profits duty according to the best of their judgment

3. Notice of an assessment shall be served on the person charged or on the person in whose name he is charged

4. A notice of assessment under the act may be delivered to the person on whom it is intended to be served, or served upon him by post

Service by post in this regulation shall have the same meaning as in the Interpretation Act, 1889.

5 Any person dissatisfied with the amount of any assessment made upon him may at any time within 30 days from the date of the service of notice of assessment, or within such further time as the commissioners of inland revenue may allow, give notice to the surveyor of taxes named in the notice of assessment of his intention to appeal against the amount of the assessment, and every such notice shall specify the grounds of appeal, and, in England, Scotland, and Wales, whether the appellant desires that the appeal shall be heard by the general commissioners or the special commissioners

6. With reference to any notice of appeal and to the hearing of an appeal, the general or special commissioners as the case may be shall subject to the provisions of the act, and to any regulations made thereunder. have all such powers in relation to any matter of appeal as are possessed by them in relation to notices of appeal and the hearing of appeals under any act for the time being in force relating to income tax. The general or special commissioners shall certify in writing to the appellant and to the commissioners of inland revenue after determining any appeal their decision and the amount if any. by which any assessment has been thereby altered

7. The commissioners of inland revenue may be represented on the hearing of an appeal by any person nominated in that behalf by them, and any person so nominated shall have the same powers with reference to appeals as may for the time being be exercised by a surveyor of taxes with reference to appeals relating to income tax.

8 A surveyor of taxes may for any purpose in connection with the assessment and collection of the duty and the hearing of appeals make use of or produce in evidence any returns correspondence, schedules, accounts statements or other documents to which he has had or may have lawful access for the purposes of income tax, and shall have the same right to examine all accounts schedules and statements furnished to the general or special commissioners as he has in the case of appeals relating to income tax.

9. Any barrister or solicitor or member of an incorporated society of accountants may be heard by the general or special commissioners on an appeal.

10. No commissioner interested in his own right or in the right of any other person, in any matter under appeal shall take part in or be present at the hearing or determination thereof.

11. The commissioners of inland revenue may make additional assessments in any case where they deem it necessary at any time within three years from the date of the first assessment.

Provided That no such additional assessment shall be made in any case where an assessment has been reduced by the general or special commissioners upon an appeal or by any court by which an appeal has been reheard.

12. Any notices required to be given to the commissioners of inland revenue may be given either to the commissioners at their principal office in London or to the surveyor of taxes acting for the district in which the person giving such notice resides or carries on business.

13. In these regulations unless the context otherwise requires the expression "surveyor of taxes" means a surveyor as defined by the Taxes Management Act. 1880, and "the act" means the Finance (No. 2) Act, 1915

SCHEDULE

Income Tax Act, 1842 (5 and 6 Vict., c. 35)
  Section 40
  Section 41, save in so far as it relates to a married woman.
  Section 44.
  Section 51, save in so far as it relates to a married woman.
  Section 100, Schedule D. Rules applying to the first and second cases of that schedule. Rule 3, down to and including the words "and no separate statement shall be allowed in any case of partnership."
Taxes Management Act, 1880 (43 and 44 Vict., c. 19)
  Section 15, subsections (2) and (5)
  Section 55 down to and including the words "the several particulars on which the charge is made"
Finance Act, 1907 (7 Ed. 7, c. 13)
  Section 22, subsection (2)
Finance Act 1914 (4 and 5 Geo. 5, c. 10)
  Section 10, subsection (2)
Finance (No. 2) Act, 1915 (5 and 6 Geo. 5, c. 89):
  Section 31.

MEMORANDA BY THE BOARD OF INLAND REVENUE, AUGUST, 1917.

VALUATION OF STOCKS.

The board of inland revenue are prepared to adopt the following modifications of the general principle that stocks should be valued at cost price or market value, whichever is the lower

1. *Final valuation—General concession for excess-profits duty.*—A period of two years will be allowed after the termination of the war in which to ascertain by actual realization the value of the stock appearing in the account at the end of the last accounting period, and an allowance made from the profits of that period for any difference between the valuation and the sum realized

The loss (if any) on only such stocks as were in hand at the end of the last accounting period will be brought into the adjustment, but the whole of such stocks, not individual parcels selected by the taxpayer, must be considered

The necessary sanction for this modification of general principles will be given by a regulation under section 40, subsection 3, of the Finance (No. 2) Act, 1915.

2. *Treatment of "Base stocks."*—Certain classes of industry require to keep stocks of raw or semimanufactured goods for the purposes of manufacturing processes, and these goods are frequently of such an imperishable character that a minimum quantity required for a business could be held untouched for a long period.

Accordingly any class of trade—

(*a*) Which requires for its manufacturing processes to keep such stocks, and
(*b*) In which a recognized practice has obtained of valuing a constant quantity at a fixed price, the board of inland revenue are prepared to recognize the practice.

The board of inland revenue would regard goods as imperishable which are of sufficient durability to last without material deterioration during a period equal to the length of the war.

Any individual member of the class who has not adopted the method in his business may be allowed to do so for the purposes of excess-profits duty, but may not claim as the constant quantity of stock so valued a greater quantity than the minimum amount held at any stock taking in the three prewar trade years.

Where a claim is made that an industry should be brought within this concession, the board of inland revenue are prepared to receive representations and to consider evidence as to the existence of a material body of such practice in the industry and as to the character of the stocks to which it is claimed the method should be applied, with a view to securing the uniform treatment of all members of the industry.

The balance of stock above the minimum quantity in cases falling under this modification of the general principle is to be treated as in (1).

3. *Replacement of minimum quantities in certain circumstances.*—Profits derived from sales which reduce stock below the particular minimum or constant quantity adopted for any business are not the less trading profits. Where, however, a raw material is associated with plant in a manufacturing process (e. g., metal kept to a constant level in galvanizing baths), the board of inland revenue will consider a claim under section 40 (3) of the Finance (No. 2) Act, 1915, that it is akin to a capital asset, like plant, which has been exceptionally depreciated (by depletion) or of which the renewal has been postponed.

4. *Hidden stock reserves generally.*—Where in an industry or as respects a class of stock to which the foregoing (2) does not apply, the owner of a business has taken a quantity of stock at a base price, the stock will fall to be valued during the periods of liability at cost or market value, whichever is the lower: but from the final valuation (on that basis) there will be allowed a deduction of a sum (in pounds sterling) equal

to the original difference (at the end of the standard period) between the valuation on the base method and a valuation on the cost or market value method. Alternatively, the first stock valuation may be revised and put upon the general basis of cost or market value, when the modification outlined in (1) will apply.

WEAR AND TEAR AND SPECIAL DEPRECIATION AND OBSOLESCENCE ALLOWANCES

1. *Basis of profits for excess-profits duty purposes*.—Excess-profits duty is chargeable, generally speaking, by reference to profits which are computed on income-tax principles; but the temporary character of the duty and its relation to the existing war conditions have rendered necessary special allowances for depreciation in the value of assets, additional to the allowances granted for income-tax purposes. It is the purpose of this memorandum to explain shortly the nature and extent of these various provisions in the case of excess-profits duty, and more particularly their practical application to the profits of a manufacturing business.

2. *Statutory allowances*.—So far as income tax is concerned, it is well known that allowances are restricted to the diminution in value due to wear and tear of plant and machinery (sec 12 of Customs and Inland Revenue Act, 1878) For excess-profits duty purposes, on the other hand, further allowances are admissible. Section 40 (3) of the Finance (No. 2) Act, 1915, provides for special relief being granted in respect of—

(*a*) Postponement or suspension, as a consequence of the present war, of renewals or repairs,

(*b*) Exceptional depreciation or obsolescence of assets employed in the business due to the present war; and

(*c*) The necessity in connection with the war of providing plant which will not be wanted for the purposes of the trade or business after the termination of the war.

3. *The measure of special depreciation and obsolescence allowances*.—These allowances extend to any material assets employed in a business and not merely to machinery and plant Where these assets have been constructed or acquired during the war at an inflated price and will sink to a lower level of value, or even to scrap value, at the end of the war, full relief can be claimed. The measure of the allowance to be made in respect to such assets will be the difference between cost and postwar value. An allowance of the like nature is, of course, applicable also to assets in use before the war, the value of which has fallen owing to war causes. The measure of the allowances in such cases is the difference between the value of the assets (depreciated or written down for wear and tear) at the date when liability to excess-profits duty began and their postwar value.

4. *Determination of special depreciation allowances*.—Inasmuch as postwar value and the duration of the war are unknown, the board of inland revenue have been unable in most cases to make final allowances of the foregoing character, but where the necessary evidence is furnished that depreciation is taking place or is inevitable at the end of the war, they are ready to make provisional allowances subject to subsequent correction.

5. *Period over which special depreciation allowances fall to be granted*.—As a general rule these allowances, whether provisional or final, will be "spread," i. e., granted by installments in successive accounting periods during the lifetime of the duty, but in exceptional cases where new assets are being regularly acquired during successive accounting periods, and the taxpayer desires that the allowance (whether provisional or final) for each asset or group of assets should be wholly or mainly granted in the accounting period in which the asset is acquired, the board will not object to that course being taken.

6. "*Controlled*" *firms*.—Where in the case of businesses which are "controlled" under the Munitions of War Act, 1915, allowances of the foregoing character for depreciation or obsolescence have been determined by the minister of munitions for purposes of the munitions levy, the amounts so ascertained have been adopted by the board of inland revenue for excess profits duty purposes. The repeal of the munitions levy as at 31st December, 1916, and the transfer to the board of inland revenue of the duty of assessing and collecting the levy (up to that date)—recently enacted by the Finance Act, 1917—involve an alteration of existing arrangements to the extent that depreciation allowances not already ascertained by the ministry of munitions will fall to be determined by the board of inland revenue, who have made arrangements to secure continuity of practice in the methods of granting the allowance

7. *Appeals as to special depreciation allowances*.—Where a taxpayer is dissatisfied with the allowances granted by the board of inland revenue in respect of special depreciation or obsolescence of assets, he may require his case to be referred to the board of referees appointed under Part III of the Finance (No 2) Act, 1915, or—in the case

of a "controlled" firm—to the board of referees appointed under the Munitions of War Act, 1915

8 *Wear and tear allowance* —For excess profits duty, the allowance for wear and tear of plant and machinery will usually be similar to the allowance granted under the Income Tax Acts Its amount is to be that reasonably and properly attributable to the accounting period (Finance (No 2) Act, 1915, fourth schedule, Part I, rule 3). The income tax allowance for wear and tear (which is fixed by the income tax commissioners) is not limited by statute to any specific amount or rate, the only provision being that it shall represent the diminished value of the plant and machinery by reason of wear and tear during the year Where for any special reason it is claimed that the allowance for wear and tear of machinery and plant should, for excess profits duty, exceed that allowed for income tax, application should be made in the first instance to the surveyor of taxes dealing with the excess profits duty assessment An appeal on the question may be made either to the district commissioners of taxes or to the special commissioners

9. *Wear and tear allowance immaterial in certain circumstances* —Generally speaking, the ordinary allowance for wear and tear in the case of excess profits duty is of comparatively small importance in so far as it relates to plant and machinery which may be the subject of an allowance for special depreciation owing to the war as explained above In such cases the difference between war value and postwar value necessarily includes the ordinary allowance for wear and tear

10. *Deferred renewals and repairs* —As regards the allowance authorized for the postponement or suspension, as a consequence of the war, of renewals or repairs, the amount admissible is usually capable of estimation and agreement when an excess-profits duty assessment is made The taxpayer has the right of appeal to the board of referees appointed under Part III of the Finance (No. 2) Act, 1915, or, in the case of a "controlled" firm, to the board of referees appointed under the Munitions of War Act, 1915

11 *Special points.*—Reference may also be made to the following points on which questions sometimes arise

(*a*) *Obsolete machinery* —Where prewar machinery or plant has become obsolete from causes not actually relating to the war but arising during the war, and is then replaced, an allowance for the difference between the written-down value and the scrap value is admissible, and where the replacement is not effected during the war, but shortly after, a like allowance may be claimed under section 40 (3) of the Finance (No. 2) Act, 1915

(*b*) *Depreciation of prewar buildings* —Special depreciation of prewar buildings due to the war may be allowed for under the same subsection. Normal depreciation taking place equally in the past and in the present, if allowed, would not, in most cases, affect the liability to excess profits duty.

(*c*) *Special purchases of machines, etc* —It will happen from time to time that a manufacturer will purchase machines, etc., for the purpose of specific contracts and will wish, from motives of prudence, to write down the value of the machines to a low figure out of the profits of the contracts. In cases in which purchases of this character have regularly occurred, both in the past and in the present, the nonallowance of a special depreciation beyond the ordinary wear and tear allowance would not normally affect the liability to excess-profits duty. Where, on the other hand, purchases of this kind take place only during war periods, they would usually be attributable to war conditions, in which event a special allowance can be claimed under section 40 (3) of the Finance (No. 2) Act, 1915

FORM OF RETURN.

RETURN OF PROFITS OF THE TRADE OR BUSINESS AND OTHER PARTICULARS IN CONNECTION THEREWITH.

(a) Full style or designation of the trade or business	(a)	
(b) Names and addresses of the partners, in the case of a firm	(b) Names	Addresses
(c) Nature of the trade or business	(c)	
(d) Where carried on.	(d)	
(e) Whether the accounts of the trade or business have been made up; and, if so—	(e)	

(f) The commencing and ending dates of the accounting period or periods ended after , 191 , for which the accounts have been made up.	See notes 1 and 2 on sheet enclosed	(f) Accounting period commencing on , 191 , and ending on , 191 .	Accounting period commencing on , 191 , and ending on , 191 .	Accounting period commencing on , 191 , and ending on , 191 .	Accounting period commencing on , 191 , and ending on , 191 .	[NOTE — where there are more than four such accounting periods, further forms will be supplied on application to the before-mentioned surveyor of taxes.]
(g) Amount of profits arising from the trade or business in each of the above accounting periods, computed as the acts direct	See note 1 on sheet enclosed.	(g) £	£	£	£	
†(h) Amount of profits arising from the trade or business in each of the three last prewar trade years (i. e., the three last trade years which ended before August 5, 1914) computed as the acts direct.	See notes 4, 5, and 6 on sheet enclosed	(h) Year ended 191 . £	Year ended 191 . £	Year ended 191 . £		

PARTICULARS REQUIRED TO BE TRANSMITTED WITH THIS RETURN.

(1) Copies of any original trading accounts and profit and loss accounts for each of the above accounting periods and for each of the three last prewar trade years, and of any original balance sheets as at the end of each of the said periods and years and as at the commencement of the first of the said prewar trade years.

NOTE.—In so far as copies complying with this requirement have already been furnished for the purpose of income tax or excess-profits duty, it should be so stated, and duplicate copies need not be transmitted. Moreover, if the profits of each accounting period, as computed by you, fall below the point involving liability to duty, copies of the accounts need not in the first instance be supplied, and in that event a subsequent intimation will be made as to any particulars required beyond those declared on the form, while if you wish to show that in the case of your trade or business the percentage standard exceeds the profits standard (see note 7), a further communication will be addressed to you specifying the particulars required in relation to the prewar standard, and no copies of accounts need be furnished with this return other than those relating to the accounting periods.

(2) Full particulars, if not already notified, as to the nature of any fictitious or artificial transaction or operation entered into or carried out, before the commencement of the acts relating to the excess-profits duty, during any of the above accounting periods or prewar trade years [See section 44 (3) of the finance (No. 2) act, 1915, quoted on page 4.]

*It will greatly facilitate agreement as to the amount of your liability if you will attach—

(i) Detailed statements showing how the amounts returned by you in spaces (g) and (h) above are arrived at from the accounts.

(ii) Detailed statements showing your computation of the amount of excess-profits duty payable by you in respect of the above accounting period or periods.

† The particulars asked for under (h) need not be repeated if already furnished in a previous return.

DECLARATION.

I hereby declare that the foregoing particulars, and the particulars transmitted herewith, are in every respect truly and correctly stated, to the best of my judgment and belief

Signature. . . . .

Date. . . . .

State whether the return is made—
On your own behalf,
or, As partner of a firm,
or, As trustee, agent, receiver, or factor, etc , and for whom;
or, As the officer of any corporation or company.
. . . .
. . . .

ALLOWANCES AND RELIEFS.

You are invited to state in the space provided on page 4 of this form, or on separate sheets accompanying the form, particulars of any allowances or reliefs claimed by you. (See division B of enclosed notes.)

CANADA.

BUSINESS PROFITS WAR TAX ACT, 1916.

[6 and 7 Geo. V. c. 11.]

As amended in 1917 (7 and 8 Geo. V, c. 6) and 1918.

AN ACT TO LEVY A TAX ON BUSINESS PROFITS.

[Assented to May 18, 1916.]

His Majesty, by and with the advice and consent of the Senate and House of Commons of Canada, enacts as follows:-

1. This act may be cited as the Business Profits War Tax Act, 1916.

2. In this act and in any regulations made under this act, unless the context otherwise requires—

(*a*) "Minister" means the minister of finance of Canada;

(*b*) "Board" means the board of referees appointed under the provisions of section 9 hereof;

(*c*) "Non-Canadian company" means an incorporated company having its head office or principal place of business outside Canada but having assets in or carrying on business in Canada, either directly or through or in the name of any other person;

(*d*) "Person" means any individual or person and any partnership, syndicate, trust, association, or other body and any body corporate, and the heirs, executors, administrators, curators, and assigns, or other legal representatives of such person, according to the law of that part of Canada to which the context extends;

(*e*) "Tax" means the tax, toll, or duty authorized by section 3 of this act;

(*f*) "Taxpayer" means any person paying, liable to pay, or suspected by the minister to be liable to pay any tax imposed by this act,

TAX IMPOSED.

3. There shall be levied and paid to His Majesty a tax of 25 per cent of the amount by which the profits earned in any business exceeded, in the case of a business owned by an incorporated company, the rate of 7 per cent per annum, and, in the case of a business owned by any other person, the rate of 10 per cent per annum upon the capital employed in such business. Such tax shall be levied against and paid by the person owning such business for each and every accounting period ending after the 31st day of December, 1914.

In any business where the said profits exceed 15 per cent per annum, the said tax shall be increased to 50 per cent with respect to all profits in excess of the said 15 per cent but not exceeding 20 per cent per annum, and where the said profits exceed 20 per cent per annum the said tax shall be increased to 75 per cent with respect to all profits in excess of the said 20 per cent, and such increases in the tax shall be levied against and paid by the person owning such business for each and every accounting period ending after the 31st day of December, 1916.

Any person having a business with a capital of not less than $25,000 and under $50,000 shall pay a tax of 25 per cent of the amount of the profits exceeding 10 per cent per annum upon the amount of the capital employed therein.

Provided, however—

AMOUNT OF OTHER WAR TAXES TO BE DEDUCTED.

(*a*) That the amount paid or payable by any person under the provisions of part 1 of the Special War-Revenue Act, 1915, and the Income War Tax Act, 1917, shall be deducted from the amount which such person would otherwise be liable to pay under the provisions of this act, and the minister shall have power to determine any questions that may arise in consequence of any difference in the several periods for which the taxes under the said acts and under this act, respectively, are payable, and the decision of the minister thereon shall be final and conclusive, but in computing the profits of his business no taxpayer shall include any taxes paid under the said acts in the expenses of his business.

DIVIDENDS FROM TAX-PAYING COMPANY EXEMPTED.

(*b*) That the dividends received from the stock of any incorporated company which has paid a tax upon its profits under the provisions of this act shall not be included when the profits of any business are being determined.

ACCOUNTING PERIOD DEFINED.

4. For the purposes of this act an accounting period shall be taken to be the period for which the accounts of the business have been made up, but where the accounts of any business have not been made up for any definite period or for the period for which they have been usually made up, or if a year or more has elapsed without the accounts being made up, the accounting period shall be taken to be such period and ending on such a date as the minister may determine.

TRADES AND BUSINESSES INCLUDED.

5. The businesses to which this act applies are all trades and businesses (including the business of transportation) of any description carried on, or partly carried on, in Canada, whether continuously or not, except—

(*a*) The business of any person the capital employed in which has been throughout the accounting period less than $25,000, other than a business which, or 20 per cent or more of which, is or has been the manufacturing or dealing in munitions of war or in materials or supplies of any kind for war purposes;

(*b*) The business of life insurance;

(*c*) The business of farming and live-stock raising; and

(*d*) The business of any company, commission, or association not less than 90 per cent of the stock or capital of which is owned by a province or a municipality.

COMPUTATION OF PROFITS.

PROFITS DEFINED

6. The profits shall be taken to be the net profits arising in the accounting period.

2. The profits of a non-Canadian company shall be the net profits arising from its Canadian business, including both domestic and export business.

3. No deductions from the gross profits for depreciation or for any expenditure of a capital nature for renewals, or for the development of a business, or otherwise in respect of the business, shall be allowed, except such amount as appears to the minister to be reasonable and to be properly attributable to the accounting period, and the minister when determining the profits derived from mining shall make an allowance for the exhaustion of the mines.

INCREASING REMUNERATION OF DIRECTORS.

4. Any deduction made from the gross profits for the remuneration of directors, managers, and persons concerned in the management of the business shall not (unless the minister, owing to any special circumstances, otherwise directs) exceed the sums deducted for those purposes in the last accounting period ending before the 1st day of January, 1915, and no deductions shall be allowed in respect of any transaction or operation of any nature where it appears, or to the extent to which it appears, that the transaction or operation has improperly reduced the amount to be taken as the amount of the profits of the business for the purposes of this act.

CONTRACTS EXTENDING OVER MORE THAN ONE ACCOUNTING PERIOD

5. In the case of any contract extending beyond one accounting period from the date of its commencement to the completion thereof and only partially performed in any accounting period there shall (unless the minister, owing to any special circumstances, otherwise directs) be attributed to each of the accounting periods in which such contract was partially performed, such proportion of the entire profits or estimated profits in respect of the complete performance of the contract as shall be properly attributable to such accounting periods, respectively, having regard to the extent to which the contract was performed in such periods.

COMPANIES NOT RECEIVING PROFIT EARNED BY ITS BUSINESS.

6. Where an incorporated company conducts its business, whether under agreement or otherwise, in such manner as either directly or indirectly to benefit its shareholders, or any of them, or any persons directly or indirectly interested in such company by selling its product or the goods and commodities in which it deals at less than the

fair price which might be obtained therefor, the minister may for the purposes of this act determine the amount which shall be deemed to be the profits of such company for any accounting period, and in determining such amount the minister shall have regard to the fair price which, but for any agreement, arrangement, or understanding, might be or could have been obtained for such product, goods, and commodities.

CAPITAL.

CAPITAL OF A COMPANY.

7. For the purposes of this act the capital employed in the business of an incorporated company having its head office or other principal place of business in Canada shall be the amount paid up on its capital stock.

2. For the purposes of this act the capital employed in the business of a non-Canadian company shall be such portion of the amount paid up on its capital stock as shall bear the same proportion to the amount paid up on its entire capital stock as the value of its assets in Canada bears to the value of its total assets.

HOW AMOUNT PAID UP ON STOCK IS TO BE DETERMINED.

3. For the purposes of this act the amount paid up on the capital stock of a company shall be the amount paid up in cash. Where stock was issued before the 1st day of January, 1915, for any consideration other than cash, the fair value of such stock on such date shall be deemed to be the amount paid up on such stock; and where stock has been issued since the said 1st day of January for any consideration other than cash, the fair value of the stock at the date of its issue shall be deemed to be the amount paid upon such stock. In estimating the value of stock issued for any consideration other than cash, regard shall be had to the value of the assets, real and personal, movable and immovable, and to the liabilities of the company at the date as of which such value is to be determined. In no case shall the value of the stock be fixed at an amount exceeding the par value of such stock.

RESERVE

4. For the purposes of this act, the actual unimpaired reserve, rest or accumulated profits, held at the commencement of an accounting period by an incorporated company, shall be included as part of its capital as long as it is held and used by the company as capital and dividends paid during an accounting period shall be considered as a reduction of unimpaired reserve, rest, or accumulated profits.

STOCK ISSUED AFTER FEBRUARY 15, 1916.

5. The minister may determine the amount of the capital for the purposes of this act, of any incorporated company issuing stock after the 15th day of February, 1916, and if, after the said 15th day of February, 1916, the capital stock of any incorporated company is

increased or additional stock is issued, or if the stock is in any way changed or reorganized in such a manner as to increase the amount of the capital for the purposes of this act, the minister may decide whether or not it is fair and proper to include such increase or any part thereof when determining the capital of such company for the purposes of this act, and the decision of the minister shall be final and conclusive.

CAPITAL OF PERSONS OTHER THAN COMPANIES.

8. For the purposes of this act the capital employed in the business of any person other than an incorporated company shall be taken to be the fair value of all assets, real and personal, movable and immovable, used in connection with such business in the accounting period.

2. Accumulated profits employed in the business shall also be deemed capital.

3. Any money or debts borrowed or incurred in connection with the business shall be deducted in computing the amount of capital for the purposes of this section.

COLLECTION OF TAX.

BOARD OF REFEREES.

9. The governor in council may appoint a board or boards of referees. A board shall consist of not more than three members and the members of a board shall jointly and severally have all the powers and authority of a commissioner appointed under part 1 of the Inquiries Act, Revised Statutes of Canada, 1906, chapter 104.

2. Every member of the board shall take an oath of office in Form I of the schedule to this act before performing any duty under this act. All affidavits made in pursuance of this subsection shall be filed with the minister.

RETURNS.

10. Every person liable to taxation under this act shall, on or before the 1st day of July in each year, without any notice or demand, deliver in duplicate to the minister a return in Form J of the schedule to this act or in such other form as the minister may prescribe covering each accounting period for which he is liable to taxation. In such return the taxpayer shall state an address in Canada to which all notices and other documents to be mailed or served under this act may be mailed or sent.

2. The return, in the case of a partnership, syndicate, association, or other body, shall be made and signed by a member or officer having a personal knowledge of the affairs of such partnership, syndicate, association, or other body, or, in the case of a company, by the president, secretary, treasurer, or chief agent having a personal knowledge of the affairs of such corporation, or in any case, by such other person or persons, employed in the business liable, or suspected to be liable, to taxation as the minister may require.

3. The minister may at any time enlarge the time for making any return.

11. If the minister, in order to enable him to make an assessment, desires further information, or if he suspects that any person who has not made a return is liable to taxation hereunder, he may, by registered letter, require additional information or a return containing such information as he deems necessary to be furnished him within 30 days.

2. The minister may require the production, or the production on oath, by the taxpayer or by his agent or officer of any letters, accounts, invoices, statements, and other documents, account, and other books relating to the business of any taxpayer liable, or suspected to be liable, to taxation under this act.

PENALTIES.

12. For every default in complying with the provisions of the two next preceding sections the taxpayer and also the person or persons required to make a return shall each be liable on summary conviction to a penalty of $100 for each day during which the default continues.

2. Any person making a false statement in any return, or in any information required by the minister, shall be liable on summary conviction to a penalty not exceeding $10,000 or to six months' imprisonment, or to both fine and imprisonment.

ASSESSMENT BY MINISTER.

13. The minister shall, on or before the 1st day of September in each year, or on or before such other date as he may in any case or cases prescribe, determine the several amounts payable for the tax, and shall thereupon send, by registered mail, a notice of assessment in such form as the minister may prescribe to each taxpayer notifying him of the amount payable by him for the tax. The tax shall be paid each year within one month from the date of the mailing of the notice of assessment.

In default of payment, interest at the rate of 7 per cent per annum shall be paid on such tax until the said tax and interest are paid.

2. The minister shall not be bound by any return or information supplied by or in behalf of a taxpayer, and notwithstanding such return or information, or if no return has been made, the minister may determine the amount of the tax to be paid by any person.

LIABILITY TO PAY TAX CONTINUES FOR THREE YEARS.

3. Any person liable to pay the tax shall continue to be so liable for the period of three years from the time at which such tax would have been payable, and in case any person so liable shall fail to make a return as required by this act, or shall make an incorrect or false return, and does not pay the tax in whole or in part, the minister may at any time within the said three years assess such person for the tax, or such portion thereof as he may be liable to pay, and may prescribe the time within which any appeals may be made under the provisions of this act from the assessment or from the decision of the board.

4. The tax may be assessed on any person for the time being owning or carrying on the business or acting as agent for that person in

carrying on the business, or, where a business has ceased, on the person who owned or carried on the business or acted as agent in carrying on the business immediately before the time at which the business ceased, and where there has been a change of ownership of the business, the minister may, if he thinks fit, take the accounting period as the period ending on the date on which the ownership has so changed and assess the tax on the person who owned or carried on the business or acted as agent for the person carrying on the business at that date.

INFORMATION NOT TO BE DISCLOSED.

14. No person employed in the service of His Majesty shall communicate or allow to be communicated to any person not legally entitled thereto any information obtained under the provisions of this act, or allow any such person to inspect or have access to any written statement furnished under the provisions of this act. Any person violating any of the provisions of this section shall be liable on summary conviction to a penalty not exceeding $200.

ASSESSMENT APPEALS.

COURT OF REVISION

15. The board shall act as a court of revision, and shall hear and determine any appeal made by a taxpayer under this act in such place in Canada as the minister may direct.

NOTICE OF APPEAL

16. Any person objecting to the amount at which he is assessed, or as having been wrongfully assessed, may, personally or by his agent, within 20 days after the date of mailing of the notice of assessment, as provided in section 13 of this act, give notice in writing to the minister in Form K of the schedule to this act that he considers himself aggrieved for either of the causes aforesaid, otherwise such person's right to appeal shall cease and the assessment made shall stand and be valid and binding upon all parties concerned, notwithstanding any defect, error, or omission that may have been therein, or in any proceeding required by this act or any regulation hereunder: *Provided, however*, That the minister, either before or after the expiry of the said 20 days, may give a taxpayer further time in which to appeal.

HEARING AND DECISION BY BOARD.

17. The board, after hearing any evidence adduced and upon such other inquiry as it considers advisable, shall determine the matter and confirm or amend the assessment accordingly. The board may, in any case before it, increase the assessment. The board shall send a copy of its decision by registered mail to the taxpayer or his agent or officer. In any case where the appeal is unsuccessful the board may direct that the person who appealed shall pay the costs or part of the costs of such appeal, and if such appeal is successful the board may recommend that the costs or any part thereof be paid by the Crown.

2. The tariff of fees in force in the exchequer court of Canada shall apply to such appeals.

18. If the taxpayer fails to appear, either in person or by agent, the board may proceed ex parte or may defer the hearing.

19. If the taxpayer is dissatisfied with the decision of the board he may, within 20 days after the mailing of the decision, give a written notice to the minister in Form L of the schedule to this act that he desires to appeal from such decision. If the taxpayer gives such notice, or if the minister is dissatisfied with the decision, the minister shall refer the matter to the exchequer court of Canada for hearing and determination in Form M of the schedule to this act, and shall notify the taxpayer by registered letter that he has made such reference. On any such reference the court shall hear and consider such matter upon the papers and evidence referred and upon any further evidence which the taxpayer or the Crown produces under the direction of the court, and the decision of the exchequer court thereon shall be final and conclusive.

EXCLUSIVE JURISDICTION OF EXCHEQUER COURT.

20. Except as hereinafter expressly provided, the exchequer court shall have exclusive jurisdiction to hear and determine all questions that may arise in connection with any proceeding taken under this act, and may award costs in connection therewith.

NO ASSESSMENT TO BE SET ASIDE FOR TECHNICAL REASONS

21. No assessment shall be set aside by the board or by the court upon the ground that there has been any error or omission in connection with any proceedings required to be taken under this act or any regulation hereunder, but such board or court in any case that may come before it may determine the true and proper amount of the tax to be paid hereunder.

TAX A DEBT DUE CROWN

22. The tax and all interest and costs assessed or imposed under the provisions of this act shall be recoverable as a debt due to His Majesty from the person on whom it is assessed or imposed.

RECOVERY OF TAX, ETC.

23. Any tax, interest, costs, or penalty that may be assessed, recovered, or imposed under this act may, at the option of the minister, be recovered and imposed in the exchequer court of Canada or in any other court of competent jurisdiction in the name of His Majesty.

TAX, ETC., LIEN.

24. Taxes, interest, costs, and penalties imposed under this act shall be a lien and charge upon the property, whether real or personal, movable or immovable, of the person liable to pay the same.

REGULATIONS

25. The minister may make any regulations deemed necessary for carrying this act into effect.

DURATION OF TAX

26. The provisions of section 3 of this act shall not continue in force after the 31st of December, 1918.

Provided, however, That with respect to every business liable to taxation hereunder the period for which the returns shall be made and during which it shall be liable for assessment shall be at least 48 months, commencing with the beginning of the first accounting period ending after the 31st day of December, 1914, or for such less period as the business may have been carried on from the beginning of the said accounting period to the end of the period for which the said tax may be levied under this act.

Provided also, That the tax payable in respect of any business with a capital of not less than $25,000 and under $50,000 shall be payable for all accounting periods commencing after the 31st day of December, 1917.

SCHEDULE.

FORM I—*The business profits war-tax act, 1916.*

I, ... make oath and swear that I will faithfully and honestly fulfill the duties which devolve upon me as a member of a board of referees under the business profits war-tax act, 1916.

Sworn before me this ...... day of ......, A. D. 19...

FORM J.—*The business profits war-tax act, 1916.*

FOR PERSONS OTHER THAN INCORPORATED COMPANIES

Name of taxpayer	Address	Address in Canada to which notices, etc., may be sent	Capital employed in business.	Money borrowed and debts due by taxpayer in connection with business	Gross profits	Net profits	Accounting period
....	....	....	....	....	....	....	....

(Signature:) ....

FOR INCORPORATED COMPANIES.

Name of company.	Address of head office.	Bonds, including debenture stock.	Capital stock paid up.		Unimpaired reserve, rest, or accumulated profits.	Total of paid-up stock, reserve, rest, and accumulated profits.	Gross profits.	Net profits.	Accounting period	Value of assets in Canada.[1]	Value of assets outside Canada.[1]	Profits of Canadian business[1]
			Preferred.	Common.								
....	....	....	....	....	....	....	....	....	....	....	....	....

[1] This information only required from companies having their head office or other place of business outside Canada.

(Signature:) ....
(Rank of official.)

Address in Canada to which notices, etc., may be sent: ....

FORM K.—*The business profits war tax act, 1916*

In the matter of the assessment of..

To the MINISTER OF FINANCE

I hereby give notice that I object to the amount at which I am assessed for the following reasons

(Here shortly describe reasons.)

or I am not liable to taxation under the above act for the following reasons:

(Here shortly describe reasons.)

Dated this......day of...................... 19..

(Signature.) ....

FORM L.—*The business profits war tax act. 1916.*

In the matter of the assessment of..

To the MINISTER OF FINANCE

I hereby give notice that I am dissatisfied with the decision given by the board of referees in this matter for the following reasons:

(Here shortly describe reasons.)

and that I desire to appeal to the exchequer court of Canada.

Dated this......day of...................., A. D. 19..

FORM M.—*The business profits war tax act, 1916.*

In the matter of the assessment of..

By virtue of the powers vested in me in this behalf under the business profits war tax act, 1916, I hereby refer the appeal of............................(or my appeal) against the decision of the board of referees to the exchequer court of Canada for adjudication thereon and inclose herewith the said decision and the other papers relating to the matter.

Dated this......day of....................A. D. 19..

........................,

Minister of Finance.

To the REGISTRAR OF THE EXCHEQUER COURT OF CANADA.

FRANCE.

EXCESS-PROFITS TAX LAWS, 1916-1917.

Part I (Secs. 1-21) of Law of July 1, 1916.

(Journal Officiel, July 2, 1916.)

SPECIAL TAX ON EXCESS OR EXTRA PROFITS MADE DURING THE WAR.

Section 1. There is hereby imposed a special tax on excess or extra profits made between August 1, 1914, and the end of the twelfth month following the cessation of hostilities, by—

All unlicensed persons, excepting farmers selling their crop to the Government, who, whether directly or as subcontractors, sell supplies to be used by the Government or any public authority, and by all persons who, incidentally or aside from their regular occupation, shall have executed any business transaction of the same nature;

All persons, whether licensed or not, who give pecuniary aid or use their influence for a consideration, allowance, or commission to close a business transaction with the Government or any public authority;

All companies and persons liable to the business-license tax whose profits exceed the normal profits;

All operators of enterprises subject to the proportional royalty provided by section 33 of the act of April 21, 1810.[1]

DETERMINATION OF TAXABLE PROFITS.

Sec. 2. The special tax shall be computed by taking as a basis the excess of the net profits made during the period extending from August 1, 1914, to December 31, 1915, and during each subsequent year, respectively, over the normal profits, which shall be taken to be the average of the net profits made during the three trade years preceding August 1, 1914.

If the period prior to August 1, 1914, during which business operations, as defined in section 1, have been carried on by a taxable person is less than three years, the normal profits shall be taken to be the average profits during such period.

The normal profits shall in no case, even if the taxable person has not carried on business operations prior to August 1, 1914, be taken to be less than 5,000 francs, nor less than 6 per cent on the actual paid-up capital invested in his business, as shown by contracts, regularly kept account books, or other convincing evidence.

The normal profits and the war-time profits to be compared shall be determined by adding together the net profits of the different

[1] Mine owners pay to the State a fixed royalty and a royalty proportional to their profits.

businesses carried on in France by the same taxable person, deducting, if necessary, losses due to a deficit in any of these businesses.

For the period between August 1, 1914, and December 31,1915, the profits shall be compared with the normal annual profits increased by five-twelfths.

In comparing the profits made during the last assessment period with the normal profits, the latter, if necessary, shall be increased or diminished by a number of twelfths equal to the difference between the number of months included in said period and a trade year.

SEC. 3. The net war-time profits shall be calculated by making out the balance sheet for each enterprise according to the rules previously applicable to said enterprise, deducting particularly, if necessary, the amount required for the legal reserve and the amounts regularly reserved for amortization of buildings and material.

Subject to the revision provided in paragraph 3 of section 15, the following amounts shall also be deducted from the excess profits, reckoned as aforesaid, to obtain the taxable profits—

1. The amounts set aside for extra amortizations necessitated by exceptional depreciation of material due to lengthening of the normal daily hours of work, whether on account of installations or on account of special expenditures made for war supplies;

2. Amounts equal to 6 per cent on the capital used in plants located in invaded territory or wrecked, plus the regular amortization of said plants.

No deduction shall be allowed to an agent who has assigned a contract and collected commission in advance.

RETURNS.

SEC. 4. Within two months of the sixtieth day after the passage of this act, every taxable person, who is designated in paragraphs 2 and 3 of section 1, shall make out a return showing the excess profits made by him during the period extending from August 1, 1914, to December 31, 1915, as a purveyor or agent, deducting 5,000 francs, and showing how said profits were made.

The same return shall be made out for the following years within three months after December 31 of each year.

SEC. 5. Every holder of a business license and every mine operator designated in paragraph 4 or 5 of section 1, subject to the tax imposed by this act, shall make out, for the periods indicated, and within the time limits specified in the preceding section, a return showing, for each of his enterprises—

1. The net profits made during the period covered by the assessment;

2. The amount of the normal profits;

3. The difference constituting the excess profits;

4. The amounts deducted for the legal reserve and the regular amortizations in pursuance of paragraph 1 of section 3.

If he is unwilling or unable to supply the data requisite for determining the normal profits, he shall estimate the latter at an amount equal to thirty times the principal of the license; provided, however, that said amount shall in no case be less than 5,000 francs or 6 per cent on the capital actually invested in the enterprises.

The taxable person shall also state in his return, if necessary, the amounts to be deducted from the excess profits—

1. On account of the losses in operation designated in paragraph 4 of section 2;

2. On account of the deductions authorized by paragraphs 2ff. of section 3.

When the net profits made during the period covered by the assessment do not exceed the amount of the normal profits, the taxable person may make a merely negative return.

SEC. 6. The time limits within which the returns must be made, as provided in section 5, may be extended by decision of the director general of direct taxes at the request of a taxable person whose accounting year does not coincide with the calendar year.

In the case designated in the preceding paragraph, as in the case of the period between August 1, 1914, and December 31, 1915, the excess profits shall be calculated by using the two balance sheets which relate to the trade year to be assessed, taking from each of said balance sheets the number of months included in the trade year to be assessed.

Aside from the cases above designated, a decree shall define the circumstances in which extra time may be granted to taxable persons who, whether mobilized or not, are unable to make their return within the time and according to the conditions prescribed in sections 4 and 5.

The returns shall be made on or in accordance with forms to be kept in the city halls, shall be duly certified by those making return, and shall be addressed to the director of direct taxes in the department in which is situated the town of actual domicile or principal place of business of the persons or corporations concerned. They may be presented by proxy. Their receipt shall be acknowledged.

EXAMINATION BY COMMISSION.

SEC. 7. The returns shall be submitted for examination to a commission which shall hold sittings at the capital of each department and which shall consist of—

The treasurer:

The director of direct taxes and land valuation;

The director of indirect taxes;

The director of register, lands, and stamps.

In each customs district the collector or a deputy designated by him shall also sit in the commission.

The bureau chief having seniority in rank shall act as chairman of the commission.

A deputy collector of direct taxes, designated by the director, shall act as secretary. He shall have the right to take part in discussions but shall not be entitled to vote.

If necessary, several commissions may be established for a single department, in pursuance of a decree of the minister of finance, who shall fix the meeting place and territory of each commission. In this case, the bureau chiefs designated above shall name an official of each of their respective bureaus to act in the commission or commissions in which they do not sit in person. In each commission the official of highest rank or seniority shall act as chairman.

The commission itself shall regulate the times of its sittings. It shall be convened by its chairman.

Decisions shall be made by majority vote. In case of a tie, the chairman shall have a casting vote.

Four members shall constitute a quorum for the rendering of decisions.

SEC. 8. The commission shall examine the returns. It may grant the interested parties a hearing and may require of them and of the national, departmental, and town officials any documents necessary for establishing the bases of taxation.

It may order audits to be conducted by either one of the financial bureaus, immediately and in the presence of the interested parties or after the latter have been duly summoned.

If the commission does not accept the return, the taxable person shall be invited, by registered letter stating the contested points, to reply within a month.

The taxable person may inform the commission by registered letter within the time limit stated above of his acquiescence or objections.

When these formalities have been complied with, the commission shall fix the bases of taxation. Within a month from the day on which he receives a notification of the statements and decision of the commission, the interested party may notify the Government that he reaffirms his return. The litigation shall then be carried to the superior commission.

SEC. 9. Any person subject to the tax, who does not make his return within the time limits prescribed by sections 4 and 5 of this act, shall, one month after a notice has been sent to him, be taxed officially (*taxé d'office*).[1]

The taxable person may reply to the notice, within the time limit hereinbefore prescribed, by the negative return provided in section 5, if he believes himself not liable to taxation.

The taxation shall be determined by the commission—

1. In the case of taxable persons not holding a license, by means of data collected by Government bureaus and especially by the investigation of contracts;

2. In the case of parties subject to the mine royalty, by comparing the net profits used as a basis for the proportional royalty for each of the assessment periods for which the tax is to be levied, with the average net profits for the three trade years prior to August 1, 1914;

3. In the case of companies required to publish their balance sheets, by comparing the balance sheets for the three trade years prior to August 1, 1914, with the balance sheet for the trade year for which assessment is to be made;

4. In the case of license holders and companies not required to publish their balance sheets, by any data at the disposal of the commission.

It may order audits to be conducted by either of the financial bureaus in the immediate presence of the interested parties or after the latter have been duly summoned.

In no case shall the normal profits be estimated at a sum less than 5,000 francs, nor less than thirty times the principal of the license, nor less than 6 per cent on the capital invested.

[1] *Taxation d'office* is a summary procedure in which the taxpayer is deprived of certain privileges and safeguards.

SEC. 10. The administration of direct taxes shall, by registered mail, notify the taxable person of the tax levied. The notice shall inform the person concerned, with respect to each of his enterprises, of the figures decided upon as constituting—

1. The profits established for the period covered by the assessment;
2. The amount deducted as normal profits;
3. The excess constituting the basis of taxation.

A taxable person on whom a tax is assessed officially may contest the assessment before the commission of appeals within the time limit allowed in section 8, only by producing all evidence calculated to prove the exact amount of his excess or extra profits.

In the case of the enterprises designated in paragraph 5 of section 1, the taxable profits shall be ascertained from the net profits used as a basis for the proportional royalty.

APPEALS.

SEC. 11. Within a month after they have received notification of the decisions of the commission of first instance, the persons or corporations concerned may appeal from said decisions.

Within the same period, the director of direct taxes may appeal from any decision of the commission which he may judge derogatory to the rights of the treasury.

These appeals shall be carried before a superior commission which shall hold sessions in the ministry of finance, and shall comprise—

A chairman of a committee of the council of state, designated by the minister of justice, who shall act as chairman[1] of the commission;

Two councillors of state in the regular service, likewise designated by the minister of justice;

Two master counsellors at the court of accounts, designated by the minister of finance;

Two inspectors of finance, designated by the minister of finance;

The director general of direct taxes, and an administrator of direct taxes designated by the minister of finance;

Six members designated by the assembly of presidents of chambers of commerce, or in case said assembly takes no action, by the minister of commerce and industry;

Auditors to the council of state, designated by the minister of justice, and auditors to the court of accounts designated by the minister of finance, may be attached to the commission as reporters.

One or more senior employees of the general director of direct taxes designated by the minister of finance shall act as secretary or secretaries.

The superior commission may be divided into two committees, each of which shall include, besides the council of state committee chairman, one councillor of state, one master counsellor at the court of accounts, one inspector of finance, one of the two direct taxes officials designated by the minister of finance, and three of the members designated by the presidents of chambers of commerce or, as hereinbefore provided, by the minister of commerce and industry.

The superior commission shall render decision on briefs. Its decisions, which shall be accompanied by opinions, shall be final.

---

[1] See also amendment in sec. 8 of the law of Dec. 31, 1917, *infra*.

They may be contested before the council of state solely on the ground that the commission has exceeded its authority or violated the law.

The operation of the commission and the organization of the committees hereinbefore provided shall be regulated by decree.

RATE OF TAX.

SEC. 12. The tax shall be computed—

In the case of the excess profits made by the persons designated in paragraphs 2 and 3 of section 1, at the rate of 50 per cent;

In the case of the excess profits of corporations or persons subject to the license tax or the mine royalty designated in paragraphs 4 and 5 of section 1, at the rate of 50 per cent on the portion of profits in excess of 5,000 francs.

SEC. 13. When the return made by a taxable person shall be declared inadequate, the tax on the fraction of the profits not returned shall be increased by one-half, provided said fraction be more than a tenth of the total profit. In this case the burden of proof before the commission instituted by section 11 shall fall upon the Government.

However, the penalty provided in the foregoing paragraph shall not be imposed when a bona fide error has been made.

SEC. 14. The tax on the taxable profits shall be increased by 10 per cent in the case of every taxable person who does not make out a return within the time limits prescribed in section 4.

SEC. 15. Any omission detected by the administration of direct taxes may be rectified at any time up to the termination of the year following that of the cessation of hostilities.

The commission established by section 7 of this act shall determine the bases of additional taxation in accordance with the procedure prescribed in section 8, subject to the right of appeal provided in the same section.

Whenever the amounts set aside for amortizations of buildings, material, implements, or bad debts shall be declared excessive by the commission, the amount over a reasonable allowance shall be considered as excess profits realized during the last assessment year.

On the other hand, whenever a taxable person has appended a claim for rebate to his return for the last assessment year, and the said amounts shall be declared inadequate by the commission, the difference shall be chargeable to the last assessment year.

PAYMENT IN INSTALLMENTS.

SEC. 16. The procedure for making out the lists and collecting the excess-profits tax shall be the same as in the case of direct taxes.

The taxes shall be payable in four installments, each equal to one-fourth of the total amount: in the case of the period from August 1, 1914, to December 31, 1915, at bimonthly intervals beginning on the first day of the month following the publication of the list; and in the case of the other trade years, at quarterly intervals.

However, in the case of all those corporations or persons holding licenses or subject to the mine royalty who are designated in paragraphs 4 and 5 of section 1, the last two quarters of the tax for each assessment year shall be payable only after the expiration of the six months following the last trade year of the period for which the special tax shall be levied.

Within said six months, in case of deficit in comparison with the normal profits shown by any one of the balance sheets for the period of war, the taxable person shall be entitled, on producing all his tax sheets relative to the tax in question, to an abatement equal to the amount of said deficit. The abatement shall be computed by multiplying the amount of said deficit by the figure representing the average tax rate for the several trade years.

The amount of the abatement shall be deducted from the taxes remaining due for the preceding trade years; but in no case shall the same abatement be deducted more than once.

SEC. 17. Corporations, persons subject to the license tax, and [mine] operators subject to the proportional royalty provided by section 33 of the act of April 21, 1810, if they shall furnish evidence of having used, before April 1, 1916, on improvements or extension of their business, a part or the whole of the excess or extra profits taxed by the present law, may be authorized to pay the taxes on profits thus used in three annual installments, the starting point for said installments being the year in which the lists shall be issued.

Such authorizations shall be granted, after investigation of the evidence designated in the foregoing paragraph, by the commission established by section 7, subject to the right of appeal to the superior commission as provided in section 11.

For the exercise of the privilege of the treasury (*privilège du Trésor* [1]) and in applying the triennial rule, each of the three annual installments shall be considered as a separate tax for the year during which it is payable.

Notwithstanding such authorization, payment of taxes remaining due may be immediately demanded in case of dissolution of the corporation, failure or judicial liquidation, assignment or discontinuance of the business.

SECRECY.

SEC. 18. All notices and communications exchanged between the agents of the Government or addressed by them to the taxable persons concerning the special tax on excess or extra profits made during the war, shall be transmitted in sealed envelopes.

The postal franks and special franking rates found necessary shall be determined as in the case of the general income tax.

Every person called upon, by reason of his duties or official functions, to take part in levying or collecting the tax or deciding litigation arising therefrom, shall be bound to professional secrecy as defined in section 378 of the Penal Code, and liable to the penalties provided in said section.

SEC. 19. Taxable persons shall be authorized to secure extracts from the lists made out for the special tax on excess or extra profits realized during the war, in conformity with the legislative provisions and other rules governing direct taxes; but only in so far as their own assessments are concerned.

[1] A government lien on account of unpaid taxes.

PENALTIES.

SEC. 20. Every taxable person who, by the use of fraudulent means for the purpose of escaping, in whole or in part, the assessment of the tax, conceals or attempts to conceal his profits, shall be punished by imprisonment for not less than three months and not more than two years, or by a fine of not less than 500 nor more than 10,000 francs, or by both such fine and imprisonment.

Section 463 of the Penal Code [1] shall apply to contraventions of this act.

SEC. 21. The provisions of section 1167 of the Civil Code [2] shall apply to acts of fraud against the State, committed by a taxable person since January 13, 1916.

AMENDMENT IN THE BUDGET LAW OF DECEMBER 30, 1916 (§8).

(Journal Officiel, Dec. 31, 1916)

INCREASE OF TAX.

SEC. 8. The rate of the tax on excess or extra profits made during the war, which had been fixed at 50 per cent by section 12 of the act of July 1, 1916, is hereby increased to 60 per cent as to that portion of taxable profits made after January 1, 1916, which exceeds 500,000 francs.

AMENDMENT IN THE BUDGET LAW OF DECEMBER 31, 1917 (§§4–8).

(Journal Officiel, Jan. 1, 1918.)

INCREASE OF TAX.

SEC. 4. The rate to be applied under the conditions set forth in section 12 of the act of July 1, 1916, as amended by section 8 of the act of December 30, 1916, in calculating the special tax on excess or extra profits made during the war shall, as to profits made since January, 1917, be determined as follows:

Fifty per cent on that portion of taxable profits below 100,000 francs;

Sixty per cent on that portion between 100,000 francs and 250,000 francs;

Seventy per cent on that portion between 250,000 francs and 500,000 francs;

Eighty per cent on that portion exceeding 500,000 francs.

The rates hereby established shall not apply, however, during the first two budget periods, to undertakings established since January 1, 1916. Such undertakings will remain subject to the taxes imposed by the acts of July 1 and December 30, 1916.

The provisions of the above paragraph shall also be extended to cover taxable persons habitually located in the invaded territory who have carried on no business whatsoever previous to January 1, 1916.

---

[1] Penalties may be reduced on account of extenuating circumstances

[2] Creditors may contest acts of debtors which defraud the former.

SEC. 5. The provisions of next to the last paragraph of section 4 of this amendment shall apply to business concerns which become profit-sharing in conformity to Title VI of the act of July 24, 1867, as amended by the act of April 26, 1917, provided that the number of shares held by the employees equals at least one-fourth of the total number of shares of the capital stock.

In order to take advantage of the provision of this section, as well as those of the last two paragraphs of the preceding section, a special request must be made in the tax return. The commissions of first instance[1] shall pass upon such request, which, however, may be appealed to the superior commission.

SEC. 6. In reckoning the normal profits which shall serve as a basis for the tax on those profits which have been made since January 1, 1917, that percentage of the capital invested which was established by sections 2, 3 (2), 5, and 9 of the principal act for the approximate reckoning of the normal profits, shall be increased to 8 per cent in those cases and under those conditions to which the said sections apply.

SEC. 7. After the passage of this amendment the lists of the special tax established by the act of July 1, 1916, shall be set up according to the bases of assessments determined by the commission of first instance, and shall immediately become due. The taxable persons shall, however, retain their right of appeal upon the terms, in the forms and within the periods of time specified in the said act of July 1, 1916. The basis of assessment thus contested shall not be final until after the superior commission shall have handed down its decision, and it shall be revised upward or downward in accordance with such decision.

SEC. 8. Section 11 of the act of July 1, 1916, shall be amended as follows:

"Whenever the president of the section of the council of state, whose duty it is to preside over the superior commission and the two divisions of this commission, is prevented from exercising this function, his place shall be taken by the oldest of the councillors of state present at the session."

---

[1] Established by sec. 7 of the act of July 1, 1916 (q. v.)

LUXURY TAX

LUXURY TAX IN FRANCE.

SECTIONS 27–28 OF THE LAW OF DECEMBER 31, 1917.

[As amended by law of April 5, 1918.]

(Journal Officiel, Jan. 1, 1918, p. 12, Apr. 6, 1918, p. 3000.)

SEC. 27. Three months after the passage of this act a tax of 10 per cent shall be imposed on the payment of the purchase price of any merchandise, commodity, or article whatsover offered for sale at retail or for consumption, in any shape or form, by a merchant or by a person not a merchant, if such merchandise, commodity, or article is classed as a luxury.

The classes of merchandise, commodities, or articles of whatever description to be subject to the tax of 10 per cent shall be fixed by *law, on recommendation of a commission* appointed by decree.

In the case of a public sale, the registration duty chargeable on the official record of the sale shall, as to merchandise or articles of such classes, be increased to 10 per cent of the price: *Provided, however*, That such increase shall not obtain in the case of a forced sale.

Every transaction involving an article of merchandise or of luxury, whatever its price, must, if the vendor is a merchant, be entered in a trading book approved by the administration. If the vendor is not a merchant, a receipt must be given.

All the provisions [1] of the last three paragraphs of section 23 and those of sections 24, 25, and 26 of this act shall apply to the tax of 10 per cent imposed by this section.

---

[1] These provisions, which relate to a tax of 0.20 per cent established by the same act on the retail price of articles costing more than 150 francs, are as follows:

SEC. 23. * * * Payments of the purchase price of imported articles shall be liable to the tax when such articles are consigned to the consumer.

Payments of the purchase price of articles manufactured or produced in France and sent abroad shall be exempt from the tax.

Administrative orders of the minister of finance shall provide for such measures as may be required for the collection of the tax payments for imported articles and for the exemption of payments for exported articles from the tax.

SEC. 24. The tax imposed by the preceding section is payable by the purchaser or consumer at the time of the full or partial payment of the purchase price.

The collection of the tax shall be effected in the manner provided for by administrative regulations.

SEC. 25. Every merchant must keep open to the inspection of officials of the registration office or of any other special treasury representatives, both at his main establishment and at his agencies or branch houses, a special register whose form shall be determined by administrative regulations.

Refusal to show this register shall be regarded as a cause for proceedings and shall make the merchant liable to the penalties prescribed by section 5 of the act of April 17, 1906.

The administrative regulations referred to in section 21 shall specify where and when and at what office the tax is to be paid, the form of receipt to be given, as well as such other measures as may be required to carry out the provisions of this section and of sections 23 and 24.

SEC. 26. Any vendor, purchaser, or consumer contravening the provisions of sections 23, 24, and 25 of this act or of the administrative regulations shall be punishable by a fine of 6 per cent of the amount on which the tax was not duly paid: *Provided, however*, That the amount of such fine shall not be less than 50 francs.

Proceedings for the recovery of the tax shall be instituted against the vendor, without prejudice, however, to the latter's right to recover the amount from the purchaser or consumer.

The fine provided for by paragraph 1 of this section may be increased by 25 per cent on each subsequent occasion.

Contraventions may form the subject of a prosecution by employees of the registration, direct or indirect taxes departments, officials of courts of law, or police, customs or municipal customs (octroi) officers. Such persons shall be entitled to 10 per cent of the amount collected as fines.

Proceedings may not be instituted by the treasury after three years have elapsed from the date of the discovery of the offense.

Proceedings shall be instituted and sentence passed in the form provided for by section 76 of the act of April 28, 1816.

The collection of the tax shall, however, in all cases be effected by affixing stamps to the instrument of acknowledgment given by the merchant.

This tax shall not be imposed on payments for any merchandise, commodity, or article whatsoever purchased before January 1, 1918.

SEC. 28. Payments for lodging or for food or drink of any description consumed on the premises, when made to an establishment which, by reason of the class of its customers, its management, its high prices, or its importance may be regarded as an establishment *de luxe*, shall be subject to a tax of 10 per cent.

The listing of such establishments shall be effected by a departmental commission consisting of three merchants appointed by the commercial court or courts, two representatives of the trade association concerned, a nominee of the ministry of commerce, and a nominee of the ministry of finance.

The commission shall select its own chairman and decide by a plurality of votes. Four members shall constitute a quorum. Notification of each decision shall be sent to the head of the firm or establishment involved, by registered letter, for which a receipt shall be taken on delivery.

Appeal may be lodged, either by the head of the establishment or by the director of the [local] registration office, within one month from the date of such notification.

Appeals shall be heard by a higher commission consisting of:

A nominee of the ministry of commerce, chairman;

A nominee of the ministry of finance:

Three members appointed by the congress of presidents of chambers of commerce, or, failing these, by the minister of commerce;

Two members appointed by the trade associations representing the business in which the establishment under classification is engaged.

The higher commission shall base its decisions upon the evidence in writing. The validity of such decisions may not be questioned before the council of state except on the ground that the commission has exceeded its authority or acted contrary to law: *Provided, however*, That the person concerned or the director of the [local] registration office may, at the end of one year and of each succeeding year, demand that the commission reexamine the case.

A decree shall prescribe the procedure of the departmental commissions and of the higher commission.

Only such establishments as are listed and subject to the tax of 10 per cent shall be entitled to call themselves "first-class establishments" or "establishments *de luxe*" on signs or in advertisements, announcements, guides, publications, etc. Any infraction of this rule will entail reclassification of the offending establishment.

All the provisions of sections 24, 25, and 26 of this act shall apply to the tax referred to in this section.

LAW OF MARCH 22, 1918.

(Journal Officiel, p. 2641.)

SECTION 1. The merchandise, commodities, goods, or articles of any kind enumerated in Schedules A and B appended to this act are classified as luxuries and subject to the tax of 10 per cent imposed by section 27 of the act of December 31, 1917.

SEC. 2. In the computation of the tax of 10 per cent imposed by sections 27 and 28 of the act of December 31, 1917, fractions of a franc shall be left out of consideration.

Payments or charges of less than 1 franc shall be exempt from the tax, provided they are not paid on account of a larger sum.

SEC. 3. Regulations shall be issued for carrying into effect the foregoing provisions and for determining the allowances to which merchants may be entitled.

SCHEDULE A.

ARTICLES SUBJECT TO THE TAX OWING TO THEIR NATURE AND REGARDLESS OF THEIR PRICE.

1. Photographic apparatus, lenses, and accessories.
2. Passenger automobiles, their chassis and bodies.
3. Gold and platinum jewelry.
4. Billiard tables and accessories
5. Hosiery and underwear of mixed or pure silk.
6. Artistic bronzework, ironwork, and locksmith's work.
7. Horses, ponies, donkeys, mules, for pleasure purposes.[1]
8. Bric-a-brac, antiques, and all other curios.
9. Brandies, cordials, appetizers, sweet wines.
10. Sporting guns, hunting or shooting articles.
11. Live game for game preserves or for restocking purposes.
12. Harness for saddle horses
13. Fine jewelry.
14. Limited art editions of books on special paper
15. Liveries
16. Gold or platinum watches.
17. Gold, silver, or platinum ware.
18. Perfumery articles (rouge, perfumes, essences, extracts, etc.), except soaps and dentifrices.
19 Oil paintings, water colors, pastels, drawings, original sculptures. (Original works of this class sold directly by the artist are exempt from the tax.)
20. Fine pearls.
21. Pianos other than upright pianos.
22. Precious stones, natural gems.
23. Tapestry, antique or modern, of wool or silk, loom or hand woven; oriental rugs; high warp pile carpets
24 Truffles, truffled poultry and game; truffled pâtés.
25. Hunting garments and ladies' riding habits.
26 Canoes and motor boats, yachts.

SCHEDULE B

ARTICLES SUBJECT TO THE TAX WHEN THE SALE PRICE EXCEEDS THE PRICE GIVEN BELOW (PER ARTICLE).

1 Lamp shades, 10 francs
2. Clothing accessories men's or women's, 10 francs.
3. Pet animals
   Dogs, 40 francs; other animals, 10 francs.
4. Furnishings and accessories, 10 francs.
5. Knick-knacks ("*articles de Paris*"), fancy or oriental articles of whatsoever material, except those included in Schedule A, 10 francs.
6. Fancy desk articles, 10 francs
7. Smokers' articles, 10 francs.
8. Devotional articles, 10 francs
9. Bicycles, 250 francs
10. Silver jewelry, 10 francs.
11. Imitation or plated jewelry, or jewelry made of nonprecious materials, 10 francs.
12. Hosiery, underwear:
    Children's, 20 francs; men's, 40 francs; women's, 40 francs.

---

[1] Breeders not subject to the tax.

13. Brushes, combs, and other toilet articles, 10 francs.
14. Picture frames, 10 francs
15. Canes and riding whips, 10 francs
16. China and crockery
    (a) Dinner sets for 12 persons (about 116 pieces), 200 francs.
        Single piece (small), 2 francs
        Single piece (medium size), 5 francs.
        Single piece (large size), 15 francs
    (b) Complete toilet sets, 30 francs
        Single piece, 10 francs
    (c) Tea or coffee sets, 30 francs
        Single piece (small), 2 francs
        Single piece (large), 10 francs.
17. Men's hats, 20 francs
18. Women's hats, 40 francs
19. Shoes (per pair):
    Children's, 25 francs, women's, 40 francs, men's, 50 francs.
20. Chocolate, confectionery, bonbons (per kilogram), 8 francs
21. Corsets, belts, 50 francs.
22. (a) Suits or overcoats.
    Children's, 80 francs; boys', 125 francs; men's (dress suit, frock coat, cutaway), 200 francs
    (b) Sack suits for men, 175 francs.
    (c) Separate garments
    Vests, 25 francs; trousers, 50 francs; dress coat, tuxedo, frock coat, cutaway, 125 francs; sack coat, 100 francs.
    (d) Suits or coats
    Misses', 150 francs; ladies', 250 francs.
    (e) Separate garments.
    Skirts, 100 francs, waists, 80 francs
23. Blankets, quilts, eider downs, 100 francs.
24. Cutlery, scissors (per article), 10 francs.
25. Laces, embroideries:
    Per meter—machine-made, 2 francs; hand-made, 10 francs.
    By the piece—machine-made, 6 francs; hand-made, 30 francs.
26. Fans, 10 francs.
27. Artificial or sterilized flowers (per purchase), 10 francs.
28. Natural flowers, hothouse or indoor plants (per purchase), 10 francs.
29. Furs, 100 francs.
30. Gloves, per pair, 8 francs.
31. Fire irons, 100 francs.
32. Engravings, prints, art photographs, and reproductions of works of art, 100 francs.
33. Gaiters, leggings, per pair, 30 francs.
34. Games and sporting goods, 25 francs
35. Fishing tackle, 10 francs.
36. Musical instruments other than pianos (phonographs, graphophones, pianolas, and all their accessories), 150 francs.
37. Field glasses, opera glasses, lorgnettes, reading glasses, 30 francs.
38. Toys, 20 francs.
39. Lamps, bracket lamps, 50 francs.
40. Household linen:
    Sheets, 60 francs; pillowcases, 10 francs; tablecloths (per square meter), 15 francs; napkins or towels, 4 francs.
    All other articles, 4 francs.
41. Chandeliers, drop-lights, ceiling lamps, 100 francs.
42. Trunks, 100 francs.
43. Small fancy leather articles, 25 francs.
44. Furniture:
    Bedroom, parlor, dining room, or library, for the whole or each suite, 1,000 francs.
    By the piece: small, 100 francs; medium, 250 francs; large, 500 francs.
45. Mirrors:
    Hand glasses, 20 francs.
    Large mirrors (framed), 100 francs.
46. Motorcycles, side cars, cycle cars, and similar vehicles, 2,000 francs.
47. Watches other than those listed in Schedule A, 50 francs.
48. Handkerchiefs, per dozen, 18 francs.
49. Ornaments, and knick-knacks, 10 francs.

50 Goldsmiths' wares of common metals, whether or not gilt or silvered, except tableware, per piece, 15 francs
51 Umbrellas and parasols, 25 francs
52 Perfumery articles other than those classified in Schedule A
Soaps, per cake, 2 francs.
Dentifrices, per liter, 15 francs.
Toilet water, 15 francs
53 Dress ornaments of feathers, 25 francs.
54 Clocks, clock cases, timepieces, 100 francs
55 Pelts, 50 francs
56. Photographs.
Portraits, per dozen, 40 francs
Enlargements, per piece, 40 francs
57. Upright pianos and harmoniums, 1,200 francs.
58. Ornamental feathers, 10 francs.
59 Alarm clocks, traveling clocks, desk clocks, 20 francs.
60 Curtains, bed and window draperies:
Curtains or draperies, 100 francs
Double portière, 100 francs
Single portière, 60 francs.
Bed draperies, 50 francs
61. Window curtains, sash curtains, per pair, 30 francs
62 Book binding, per volume:
Octavo and smaller sizes, 10 francs; folio and quarto size, 20 francs.
63 Ribbons, trimmings, per meter, 5 francs.
64. Ladies' hand bags, 40 francs.
65 Saddlery.
Complete carriage harness, 600 francs; single piece, 150 francs.
66 Window shades, 50 francs
67. Imitation bronze ware, 10 francs.
68 Carpeting:
Rugs, 100 francs
Bedside or hearth rugs, 25 francs
Carpets, per meter: 70 cm. wide, 20 francs; of greater width, 25 francs
69. Table covers, bedspreads, 80 francs
70. Fabrics for clothing and for furniture, per square meter, 20 francs
71. Wall hangings of every description, per square meter, 5 francs.
72 Negligées, dressing gowns, pajamas, morning gowns, 80 francs.
73 Suit cases, traveling bags, 75 francs
74. Glassware and crystal ware:
(a) Large table glasses, 2 francs
(b) Small table glasses, 1 franc 50 centimes
(c) Toilet or desk articles, 10 francs
(d) Large articles, decanters, jugs, and the like, 10 francs
75 Wines:
Bottled, 5 francs; in cask, per liter, 3 francs.
76. Carriages for private use, 1,000 francs.
77 Aviaries, bird cages, 10 francs

ADMINISTRATIVE REGULATIONS.

Decree of Minister of Finance, March 29, 1918.

(Journal Officiel, pp. 2833–2834).

TITLE III.

SEC. 20. The following payments shall be entered in the special register referred to in sections 6, 7, and 8 above:[1]

1 All payments for merchandise, commodities, or articles of any description classified as luxuries and offered for sale in whatsoever manner and under whatsoever conditions at retail or for consumption,

[1] These sections contain regulations for the administration of the 0.20 per cent retail-sales tax. They provide that all merchants receiving payments subject to the tax must keep, in a special register or stub book, a serial list of such payments, including date of sale, price, brief description of the article, and amount of the tax collected from the customer, as well as full data in the case of articles returned or exchanged, and that there must be a special book or register for each cashier's desk, if there are more than one.

2. All payments for lodging or for food or drinks of any kind consumed on the premises in an establishment classed as an establishment *de luxe*.

As regards payments for lodging for food and drinks consumed on the premises, there shall be substituted for the data [1] referred to under Nos. 3 and 4 of section 7, and No. 5 of section 14, information in keeping with the nature of the commercial transactions carried on in the establishment.

SEC. 21. For the payment of the tax of 10 per cent established by sections 27 and 28 of the act of December 31, 1917, attachable stamps for the following denominations are hereby authorized: 10, 20, 30, 40, 50, 60, 70, 80, 90 centimes; 1, 2, 3, 4, 5, 6, 7, 8, 9, 10, 20, 30, 40, 50, 100, 200, 300, 400, 500, 1,000, 2,000, 3,000, 4,000, and 5,000 francs.

These stamps shall be in accordance with the form annexed to this decree.[2] Their color may be changed by order of the minister of finance. The minister of finance shall also determine the nature of such extraordinary stamps as he may consider necessary, of the same denominations as one or more of those above referred to.

SEC. 22. The provisions of sections 10 to 19[3] of this decree shall apply to the tax of 10 per cent established by sections 27 and 28 of the act of December 31, 1917.

SEC. 23. The receipt that the vendor who is not a merchant must, in accordance with the provisions of paragraph 4 of section 27 of the act above referred to, give on account of the sale of merchandise, commodities, or articles of any description offered for sale at retail or for consumption and classed as articles of luxury, must bear the tax of 10 per cent, to which it is also liable in the form of adhesive stamps to be affixed thereto.

---

[1] I. e., price and brief description of article and serial number of sale.

[2] Not reproduced.

[3] These sections, which refer to the retail-sales tax, provide that the vendor collect the tax from the purchaser, indicating collection by affixing his signature both to a stamp in the special register or stub book and to a seal on the receipt given to the customer. Articles returned or exchanged within two months of sale entitle purchaser to recovery of amount of tax from vendor, who, in turn, may recover the amount from the tax administration on submitting proof of the transaction, including a declaration by the purchaser. On the last day of each month merchants must file abstracts of their special registers or stub books, showing amount of tax collected by them during the month and amount of tax paid back by them on account of articles returned or exchanged, and they must deposit with the tax authorities at the time of filing the difference between these two amounts.

Any merchant may, upon notifying the authorities, collect the tax on his own responsibility until otherwise advised.

Provision is made for correction of errors, inspection of books, and preservation of records.

LUXURY TAX IN GREAT BRITAIN.

CLAUSES 11–13 OF THE FINANCE BILL, 1918.

[Negatived in Committee of the Whole, June 3, new bill to be introduced.]

DUTY ON ARTICLES AND PLACES OF LUXURY.

11. (1) As from the appointed date there shall be charged, levied, and paid on all payments made in respect of the purchase or supply of articles of luxury sold or supplied in Great Britain or Ireland, other than a purchase of articles by a person who is a dealer in articles of the same or a like nature buying to sell again, and on all payments made in respect of goods sold or supplied, accommodation supplied, or services rendered, at any place of luxury in Great Britain or Ireland, an excise duty (in this act referred to as "luxury duty") of an amount equal to one-sixth part of the payment:

Provided that where the total amount paid for any articl s of luxury sold or supplied to one person at the same time, or the total amount paid at a place of luxury by one person at the same time, is less than 1 shilling, luxury duty shall not be charged in respect of the payment, and where any such payment exceeds 1 shilling, luxury duty shall not be charged on any fractional part of a shilling.

(2) Luxury duty chargeable on payments made in respect of articles of luxury sold or supplied shall be recoverable from the person by whom the articles are sold or supplied, and luxury duty chargeable in respect of payments made at a place of luxury shall be recoverable from the proprietor of the place of luxury, or if it is not recoverable from that person or the proprietor, as the case may be, shall be recoverable from the person by whom or on whose behalf the payments are made.

Where the amount of the duty is less than £50, luxury duty may, without prejudice to any other means of recovery, be recovered by the commissioners of customs and excise summarily as a civil debt.

(3) In this part of this act—

The expressions "article of luxury" and "place of luxury" mean, respectively, any article or place declared from time to time by resolution of the House of Commons originating in committee of ways and means to be an article of luxury or place of luxury.

The expression "accommodation" includes lodging, stabling, and accommodation for vehicles of any description, and the expression "services rendered" includes games and sports provided.

The expression "appointed date" means as respects any article of luxury or place of luxury, such date not being earlier than two weeks or later than four weeks after the passing of a resolution declaring the article or place to be an article or place of luxury, or the passing of this act, whichever is the later, as may be fixed by the Treasury.

The expression "proprietor" in relation to a club includes any person responsible for the management of the club.

SUPPLEMENTAL PROVISIONS.

12. (1) Luxury duty shall be denoted by and collected by stamps. to be affixed to such documents at such times and in such manner as may be prescribed by regulations made by the commissioners under this section.

(2) The commissioners of customs and excise may make regulations for securing the payment of luxury duty and generally for carrying into effect the provisions of this act as to luxury duty, and in particular as to the use and cancellation of stamps, and as to the books of account to be kept by persons chargeable with luxury duty.

The provisions (including the penal provisions) of the Stamp-duties Management Act, 1891, as amended by any subsequent act, and section 65 of the Post-Office Act, 1908, shall apply to the stamps used for denoting luxury duty.

(4) An officer of customs and excise, or any person authorized in that behalf by the commissioners of customs and excise, may at all reasonable times enter any premises where he has reason to believe that articles of luxury are sold in the course of trade, or are being sold by auction, or any place of luxury, with a view to seeing whether the provisions of this act as to luxury duty or any regulations made thereunder as to luxury duty are being complied with, and may require the production of and may examine and take copies of, or extracts from, any books or documents relating to the sale or supply of articles of luxury at these premises, or relating to the sale or supply of goods, the supply of accommodation, or the rendering of services at that place of luxury.

(5) If any person—

(*a*) Contravenes or fails to comply with any regulations made by the commissioners of customs and excise with reference to luxury duty; or

(*b*) Hinders, delays, or obstructs any officer or other authorized person in the exercise of his powers or the performance of his duties in relation to luxury duty; or

(*c*) Makes any false statement or representation with intent to evade the payment of luxury duty, he shall be liable in respect of each offense to an excise penalty of £100, or, if the offense consists in a breach of a regulation relating to the payment of luxury duty or to anything to be done at the time of making or in connection with a payment chargeable with luxury duty either to that penalty or to a penalty equal to treble the amount of the duty due, at the election of the commissioners.

POWERS OF LOCAL AUTHORITY AND POLICE AUTHORITY.

13. (1) The commissioners of customs and excise may, if they think fit, by agreement in writing with any local authority or police authority, arrange for the exercise by that authority, either concurrently with the commissioners or to the exclusion of the commissioners, of any powers of the commissioners with respect to luxury duty; and, so far as required for the purpose of giving effect to any such arrangement, the provisions of this act and any regulations made thereunder with respect to luxury duty shall have effect as if the local authority or police authority and any officer authorized by

that authority were mentioned therein in addition to or substituted for the commissioners and an officer of the commissioners.

(2) If an arrangement made under this section with any local authority or police authority so provides, any penalties or costs recovered in any proceedings instituted under the last preceding section of this act or any part of those penalties or costs may, notwithstanding anything in any other act, be paid to and retained by the local authority or police authority.

(3) Nothing in this section shall confer on any local authority or police authority any special privileges of the Crown as respects legal proceedings.

(4) Any arrangement under this section may provide for the payment out of moneys provided by Parliament of any expenses incurred by the local authority or police authority in carrying out the arrangement.

(5) The expression "local authority" means, for the purposes of this provision as respects the administrative county of London, the London County Council; as respects any borough, the council of the borough; as respects any urban district with a population of over 10,000, the district council; and as respects any administrative county (excluding the area of any such borough or urban district), the county council:

Provided that where the council of any such borough (not being a county borough) or of any such urban district agree in writing with the council of the administrative county that the borough or urban district should be included in the area of the administrative county for the purposes of this section, the borough or urban district shall be so included.

(6) In the application of this section to Scotland the expression "borough" means a royal, parliamentary, or police burgh; the expression "administrative county" means a county, and references to county boroughs and urban districts shall not apply.

ORDER OF THE HOUSE OF COMMONS, APRIL 30, 1918.

(105 H. C. Deb., 1502.)

Ordered, That a select committee be appointed to consider and report what articles and places ought respectively to be classed as articles of luxury and places of luxury for the purpose of the provisions of any act of the present session which may impose a duty on payments made in respect of the purchase or supply of articles of luxury or on payments made in respect of goods sold or supplied, accommodation supplied, or services rendered, at any place of luxury:

* * * * * * *

Ordered, That it be an instruction to the committee, in preparing the list of articles of luxury, to divide it into two parts, the one of which shall contain those articles which are intrinsically articles of luxury and the other of which shall contain those articles which ought to be treated as articles of luxury if sold at or above any specified price.

Ordered, That the committee have power to appoint from outside its own body such additional persons as it may think fit to serve on any subcommittees which it may appoint, with a view to the preparation of lists of articles of luxury of any particular classes, or lists of places of luxury of any particular classes or in any particular localities.

Ordered, That the committee have power to send for persons, papers, and records.

Ordered, That five be the quorum.

CONSIDERATION IN COMMITTEE OF THE WHOLE, JUNE 3, 1918.

(106 H. C. Deb., 1270.)

LUXURY DUTY CLAUSES NEGATIVED

CLAUSE 11 (*Duty on articles and places of luxury.*)

Mr. BONAR LAW. I beg to move, in subsection (1), to leave out the words "all payments," and to insert instead thereof the words "every payment." This is a purely drafting amendment.

Amendment agreed to.

The CHAIRMAN. The next amendment, standing in the name of the hon. member for Cambridge University (Mr. Rawlinson)—to insert the words "hire purchase"—will come later in the definition clause.

Amendment made: In subsection (1) leave out the words "all payments" ["all payments made in respect of goods sold or supplied"] and insert instead thereof the words "every payment."—[*Mr. Bonar Law.*]

Mr. BONAR LAW. I beg to move in subsection (1), to leave out the words "of an amount equal to one sixth part of the payment," and to insert instead thereof the words "at the rate shown in the scale set out in the fourth schedule to this act."

Mr. LOUGH. It is difficult to follow this.

Mr. BALDWIN. May I explain that the alteration of those words is necessitated by the fact that a scale has been drawn up to keep as closely as possible to the one sixth which was sanctioned in the following resolution, and a scale was drawn up for the purpose of administering the act so that as small an amount of stamps as possible might be used for the purpose of collecting this duty. It is also, I understand, a great convenience to the shopkeeper, and will prevent a great deal of rather intricate calculation.

Sir C. HENRY. My right hon. friend has surely not altered the flat rate of one sixth?

Mr. BALDWIN. It is very near to it.

Sir M. BARLOW. I have an amendment to this clause in its original shape, asking for a reduction in the tax, and I should like an opportunity of saying a few words in regard to it. I am not so sanguine as to assume that the chancellor of the exchequer will give us the reduction quite in the form that I suggest, but there ought to be an opportunity offered those—I speak on behalf of important organizations—who desire to make suggestions as to the amount of the tax proposed. I do not know how best in accordance with the convenience of the House and the rules of order to bring this matter forward, but the amendment would be substantially out of order, because directly the one-sixth disappears it really becomes a question of the schedule. If I could have an opportunity of dealing with the matter on the schedule—and I take it that would be the proper course—I would let the amendment as it stands drop, but I do think that an opportunity ought to be given for responsible bodies of traders to put their views before the chancellor of the exchequer and the House as to why, in their view, the tax as at present proposed is too high. I speak for a large number of associations, such as the Booksellers' Association and the Art Dealers' Association, who are not in the least hostile—I do not say that they like the tax, but they are prepared, as loyal, patriotic Englishmen, within reasonable limits to accede to the chancellor's demands—and their contention is that the burden of the tax, if you put it as high as 16⅔ per cent, will be so great that it will defeat its own purpose.

Mr HOLT. On a point of order. May I ask whether the effect of discussing the rate of the tax now will be that when we come to consider the words which the chancellor proposes to insert in the schedule we shall be debarred from any further discussion?

The DEPUTY CHAIRMAN (Sir D. Maclean). I take it that the general discussion will take place on this amendment, and of course we shall dispose of the amendment of the hon. member now in possession of the committee.

Mr. BONAR LAW. Is that amendment in order?

The DEPUTY CHAIRMAN. I shall not call upon the hon. member.

Mr. BONAR LAW. I do not know whether it is the best course, but I was going to suggest that the discussion might take place on the schedule, when it would be easy to reduce the total. It would be a pity to have the discussion twice.

Sir M. BARLOW. I am quite in the hands of the committee, and if you, Sir, agree, I am quite willing to concur.

The DEPUTY CHAIRMAN. The discussion which the hon. member wishes could be raised more correctly on the schedule.

Mr LOUGH Are we to understand that the hon member will raise this point when we come to the schedule? I would like to ask the right hon gentleman's opinion with regard to this matter We refer by this amendment to a scale, and that scale appears for the first time in the amendments now before us. The scale and certain amendments of the chancellor of the exchequer refer to a number of articles which will be sent down to us from the committee upstairs. We do not know what they will be. We are really acting in the dark. We are planning taxes and rates of taxes, and we are drawing up this working scale for a number of articles about which we do not know anything. It seems to me a very unsatisfactory way to proceed in a grave matter of this kind. Would it not be better for the chancellor of the exchequer not to move these amendments now, and for us not to go on with this part of the bill until we have the report from the committee upstairs and know exactly the articles that we are proposing to tax? It may be that the rates which we are laying down and that the principles which the chancellor of the exchequer has embodied in this and subsequent amendments may not fit any article

There may be two or three articles of gigantic importance that will come down from the committee upstairs, and we are really taking a leap in the dark in applying all these principles to the articles before we know what they are. I therefore beg to suggest to my right honorable friend, who is meeting with no obstruction of any kind to-day, that he might defer this clause of the luxury tax until we get the report of the committee, and deal with it altogether in a separate bill. It would be an objection if my right honorable friend could say that he would lose time by doing so, and would be interfering with the businesslike procedure of the House——

The DEPUTY CHAIRMAN I think it better to say that it is no use making that appeal to the chancellor of the exchequer, because you can not defer a clause which you have already amended in committee.

Mr. LOUGH Surely if the Government——

The DEPUTY CHAIRMAN I could not give my assent to it

Mr. D MASON If you were agreeable, and if it were the sense of the House that we should wait for the report of the committee, would it not be possible to defer the further consideration of this clause?

Mr BONAR LAW. I wish to say that in this matter I am entirely in the hands of the committee When we discussed this tax with my advisers, of course, it was new, and at the time that the resolutions were put down there were a lot of considerations which had not been taken into account. They have been taken into account since, and they are now embodied in the amendment before the committee The view of my advisers is that they have now covered the case, and that the general principles we have laid down will cover any schedule that is introduced At the same time, I quite realize that it is an unusual course.

My object in taking it frankly was to avoid having all the stages of two finance bills—the committee knows exactly what that means—but, in view of the way in which the House of Commons has treated every finance bill since the war began, I am perfectly certain, if that is considered to be the better method, that we can rely upon the House of Commons not wasting time and allowing us to get our bill without delay. I am in the hands of the committee, and, if there is a general feeling that it would be better to drop these luxury taxes out of this bill altogether and introduce a separate finance bill, I am perfectly ready to do it; but, if so, I wish the committee to understand that it must not be taken as in any way indicating any going back at all on the determination to carry through this proposal. It is simply a question of method. As I say, I leave myself in the hands of the committee.

Mr. MCKENNA. I think my right hon. friend has treated the House very fairly, and I am quite sure from my own experience that when he introduces his second bill the House will treat him equally fairly. I remember that in 1916 I took part of the original proposals out of the finance bill and introduced a second bill, and the House gave me the bill almost at once. I believe, after the committee has reported and we know what are the articles of luxury, that my right hon. friend will have a much easier task than he would have now that we should be legislating in the dark.

Mr. BONAR LAW I fancy from the cheers which greeted what I said, and from what my right hon. friend has said, that the committee feel that is the best method, and in these circumstances I gladly fall in with the suggestion.

Mr. HOLT. I quite agree with the course that the chancellor of the exchequer proposes to take, and I was really going to raise the same point at a subsequent stage, but I hope it is not undertsood that those who are opposed to this tax by accepting the proposal of the right honorable gentleman pledge ourselves to give a friendly passage to a bill to which we object altogether in principle.

Mr. BONAR LAW. Oh no, I do not at all expect that. All I understand it to mean is that there will be no effort except the most legitimate discussion, and that otherwise we shall be allowed to get the bill

Mr H. SAMUEL Do we understand that the first paragraph of subsection (3) will not appear in the subsequent bill when it is introduced after the committee has reported?

Mr. BONAR LAW That, of course, will come out

The DEPUTY CHAIRMAN I am sorry that I can not withdraw the clause from the committee

Mr. HOLT We can negative it

Mr. BONAR LAW. Then you will have to negative the whole clause

Mr. RUNCIMAN. If we negative the clause will that in any way interfere with the introduction of the same proposal in the form of a separate bill later in the session? We ought to have it quite clear, so that the chancellor of the exchequer is not embarrassed

The DEPUTY CHAIRMAN The decision of the committee will not affect the power to bring in another bill, it will only affect the clause in the bill.

Amendment, by leave, withdrawn

Clause, as amended, negatived

Clauses 12 (supplemental provisions as to luxury duty) and 13 (provision for enabling local authority and police authority to exercise powers in relation to luxury duty) negatived.

27566779R00074

Printed in Great Britain
by Amazon